Arthur Rackham

Books by Derek Hudson

A Poet in Parliament: The Life of W. M. Praed
Thomas Barnes of 'The Times'
British Journalists and Newspapers
Norman O'Neill: A Life of Music
Charles Keene
Martin Tupper: His Rise and Fall
James Pryde
Lewis Carroll
Sir Joshua Reynolds: A Personal Study
The Forgotten King and other essays

(With Kenneth W. Luckhurst)
The Royal Society of Arts, 1754–1954

(With Anthony Goldsmith)
On the Slant: a play

DEREK HUDSON

ARTHUR RACKHAM

HIS LIFE AND WORK

CHARLES SCRIBNER'S SONS

NEW YORK

Printed in Great Britain
Library of Congress Catalog Card Number 60–12994

Contents

APPENDIXES

A Check-List compiled by Bertram Rota

List of Illustrations

The illustration of trees and birds on page 1 is from *The Springtide of Life*, 1918. The girl and the dog on page 3 are from Grimm's *Fairy Tales*, 1909 ('Fred and Kate'). The drawing on the title-page is from the title-page of *The Rhinegold and the Valkyrie*, 1910. The trees on page 8 are from *A Wonder Book*, 1921 ('The Miraculous Pitcher'). The mice on page 12 and the head-piece on page 18 are from Hans Andersen's *Fairy Tales*, 1932. The dancing figures on page 17 are from *Comus*, 1921 ('Country Dances in Ludlow Town'). The initials which begin the text chapters are from *Mother Goose*, 1913. The end-papers are from *Peer Gynt*, 1936. The sketch on the front of the case is from *The Arthur Rackham Fairy Book*, 1933.

LIST OF ILLUSTRATIONS

Foreword

'DO NOT hunt for subjects, let them choose you, not you them,' wrote Samuel Butler in the *Notebooks*. 'Only do that which insists upon being done and runs right up against you, hitting you in the eye until you do it. This calls you and you had better attend to it, and do it as well as you can.'

I cannot pretend that in writing biographies I have always followed Butler's rule. But it has happened like that more often than not. And certainly the subject of Arthur Rackham did 'run right up against me' and 'insist upon being done'. I can even remember the day when it began to 'hit me in the eye'. I was looking through a copy of *Who's Who* of 1938, and I had savoured once again my favourite entry – that of a certain potentate who is recorded as being 'an excellent horseman; a brilliant polo player; an excellent shot, and A.1 billiard player' – when, turning over a few pages, I came to 'Rackham, Arthur, R. W. S.'

There was nothing in the least egotistical about Arthur Rackham's modest entry in *Who's Who*, but the long list of books that he had illustrated served to remind me of my own childhood and of the great pleasure his work had given to me and to so many others, and it led me to wonder whether anything in the nature of a memorial volume existed. I found that it did not; and this book, which will be published twenty-one years after Rackham's death, is an attempt to fill the gap.

Any merit it may possess is due largely to the encouragement of Arthur Rackham's daughter, Mrs Barbara Edwards, who has not only lent me her father's personal records, letters, photographs, press cuttings, etc., and made available his work for illustration, but has also generously set down her own recollections of her parents, which have guided me throughout, and taken endless pains to assist me in every possible way. I am also most grateful to Mr Bernard Rackham, C.B., the artist's brother, for his kind hospitality and advice, and for permission to reproduce drawings; and to his sister-in-law Mrs Harris Rackham for similar courtesies. Rackham's nephew and niece by marriage, Professor Walter Starkie and Dr Enid Starkie, have also placed me deeply in their debt, and I remember with gratitude the help of several other members of his family. Nor should I omit to mention the enthusiasm with which Mr Dwye Evans and Mr Hugh Williamson of Heinemann's approached the project and set about the making of this handsome book.

The overwhelming response that I received to an inquiry in the Press showed conclusively that, despite changes of artistic taste and fashion, Arthur Rackham still enjoys a special place in the affections of two or even three generations, both in his own country and in America, and that his work is far from being forgotten. Those who have helped me by contributing recollections, allowing letters to be published, or in other ways, include Dr Arthur C. Hill, Mr W. E. Dawe, Mrs W. E. Wheeler, Miss Janet Seligman, Mr Humphrey Brooke (Secretary, Royal Academy of Arts), Mr James Laver, Dr Percy E. Spielmann, Miss Dorothea Braby, Mr George E. Heath, Mrs R. L. Crosley, Mr Harold Bourne, the Hon. Mrs Geoffrey Edwards, Mr F. C. Winby, Miss Margaret Andrewes, Mr Karl Kup, Miss Carolyn E. Jakeman, Mr Roland Baughman, Mr Kerrison Preston, Mr A. R. Redway, the Assistant Keeper of the Tate Gallery,

FOREWORD

Mr Owen Oliver, Mr Guy Phillips, Mr R. H. Ward, Mr Gilbert Foley, Mr Stacy Colman, Mr J. B. Oldham, Mr Gilbert Rountree, Mr Roger Lancelyn Green, Mrs Evelyn Bolckow, Miss M. Savage, Dr Eric G. Millar, Mr Sydney H. Pavière, Mr Wilfrid Robertshaw, Mr E. J. Laws, Miss Margaret Nelson (Assistant Secretary, Art-Workers' Guild), Mr John C. Oberlin, Mrs Rachel Wolton, Mrs E. Williams Bailey, and Mr Meredith Frampton, R.A. I offer my thanks to them all, and to the many others who wrote to me.

I am most grateful to Mr Bertram Rota for compiling the check-list of the printed work of Rackham, and for his advice on the book-trade aspects of the subject.

The letters from Sir James Barrie; E. V. Lucas; and Bernard Shaw are published by kind permission of Lady Cynthia Asquith; the executor of E. V. Lucas; and the Public Trustee and the Society of Authors, respectively. Extracts from a letter written by Mrs Kenneth Grahame are published by permission of the executors of the late Lord Courtauld-Thomson. I hope for the indulgence of certain correspondents of Rackham (or their representatives) from whose friendly letters I have taken brief extracts.

For their courtesy in making available original drawings for reproduction I am greatly indebted not only to Mrs Barbara Edwards, Mrs Harris Rackham and Mr Bernard Rackham, C.B., but also to the Hon. Lady Nicolson, C.H., Mr William Mostyn-Owen, Mr Peter Lazarus, and the Trustees of the Tate Gallery. Moreover, I am most grateful to Messrs Hodder and Stoughton, Messrs Methuen and Company, Messrs Harrap and Company, and Messrs Constable and Company for co-operating with my own publishers to make it possible for a wide range of Rackham's work to be represented in this book.

D. H.

Arthur Rackham

Golden the light on the locks of Myfanwy,
Golden the light on the book on her knee,
Finger-marked pages of Rackham's Hans Andersen,
Time for the children to come down to tea.

— John Betjeman

CHAPTER ONE

Beginnings

IT WOULD MAKE an unusual beginning if his biographer could state with confidence that Arthur Rackham was descended, however remotely, from a pirate. There is a touch of macabre romanticism about the idea that is attractive and could be significant; one goes on to imagine a humorously ineffective pirate, who might have stepped out of *Peter Pan*, and who spent his time sketching on the quarterdeck when he should have been boarding the enemy with his cutlass.

John Rackham was undoubtedly a pirate. He operated from Providence Island and in 1718 commanded a brigantine. Captured by a man-o'-war in 1720, he was hanged with a number of his crew at Port Royal, Jamaica, on 17th November of that year. Can we connect dishonest John with the entirely respectable branch of the family from which Arthur Rackham sprang? Links in the chain of evidence are lacking. But the theory is supported by family tradition.

For a sound beginning, however, we had better turn to Thomas Rackham, born in the Minories, London, in or about the year 1800. The Rackham family was probably of East Anglian descent. The name Rackham has been derived from the Old-English word for a rick; it may have been a tribute, say the etymologists, to a specially large rick, or to the prominence of ricks around a homestead. Be that as it may, the latter-day Rackhams were cockneys, and Arthur Rackham was proudly conscious of the fact.

Thomas Rackham, Arthur's grandfather, was a schoolmaster, who first taught in the school of his uncle William Capel in Vauxhall Walk and who opened a private school of his own in Baalzephon Street, Bermondsey, in 1832. His only brother Joseph also kept private schools, first in Kennington and afterwards in Kensington. In 1824 Thomas married Jane Harris, herself the daughter of a teacher, James Harris, whose private school was in Prospect Row, Walworth. James Harris was an agreeable character, fond of children, a member of the Philosophical Society of London and author of a school book on Algebra. There was a measure of artistic talent in the Harris family. James's brother Henry was a lithographer, and Henry's son Augustus became a drawing master at Maidstone.

Alfred Thomas Rackham, the father of Arthur Rackham, was born on 11th July 1829, in the house in Baalzephon Street, Bermondsey, and was christened at old Bermondsey Church. It was then a relatively prosperous neighbourhood, for a number of wealthy men lived in Bermondsey at their business premises. At the age of seven or eight Alfred Thomas attended lectures given by Wallis the astronomer, Dr Birkbeck and others, at the Southwark Astronomical Society. He did not go to school, but was privately taught by one Mary Sutherland, whom he later described as 'a very able woman'. Before he was fifteen, he was accepted as a junior clerk by a proctor in Doctors' Commons at a salary of £20 a year. After two years he proceeded, this time as a full clerk, to Messrs Tebbs and Sons, also proctors in Doctors' Commons, at £40 a year.

Doctors' Commons, immortalized by Dickens in *David Copperfield,* was the name given to the area south of St Paul's Churchyard, surrounding the College of Advocates in Great Knightrider Street. The College consisted of two small quadrangles wherein the Advocates (Doctors of Law) resided or had chambers. They alone had

The struggle for seats: Scenes at Oxford Circus. *Pall Mall Budget*, 19 March 1891.

the right to act as Counsel in the Ecclesiastical and Admiralty Courts which were held in the large hall of the College. On the first day of each term the court looked very gay, when, after prayers in the adjoining dining-hall, the Judge and the Advocates, in their scarlet robes as Doctors of Law, assembled with the proctors – who corresponded to solicitors in the other courts – wearing black gowns and hoods lined with white fur.

The outbreak of the Crimean War in 1854 gave A. T. Rackham a chance of advancement. In war-time the business of the Admiralty Court was greatly increased, for it had cognizance of all naval prize matters. At twenty-four, A. T. Rackham's experience in Messrs Tebbs' office stood him in good stead. He entered the Civil Service in the Registry of the Admiralty Court with a salary of £200 a year, and was soon extremely busy preparing the Declaration of War and other papers. Much was expected of him, and he did not spare himself. Once, while copying a document for the Queen's signature, he heard St Paul's clock – the 'heart of London', as Dickens called it – strike three in the morning. Having failed three times to fill the large sheet of gilt-edged paper without a mistake, he had to return to the office earlier than usual, only a few hours afterwards, to accomplish the feat.

A. T. Rackham remained in the Registry until he became Chief Clerk, moving with it first to Somerset House and then to rooms in the new Law Courts. In 1896, while still retaining the Chief Clerkship, he was appointed to the ancient office of Admiralty Marshal and Serjeant at Mace of the High Court of Justice, at £800 a year. During each of the three years of his Marshalship he took part in the annual procession of judges and officials up the central hall of the Royal Courts of Justice on the first day of the sittings after the long vacation.

In September 1861, A. T. Rackham was married to Anne, second daughter of William Stevenson, a draper of Nottingham (her grandfather was Principal of the General Baptist College). They spent a fortnight of their honeymoon at Ventnor and another fortnight in while the daylight lasted. When this was forbidden, he still managed to hide his pencil and draw on the pillows. In the nursery Arthur was healthily mischievous. He discovered a small hole under the saddle of the large dappled rocking-horse; successive nurses lost their thimbles; and, when the children rode the rocking-horse, a mysterious and increasing rattle sounded from the interior. A note to Arthur from his grandmother Stevenson when he was nine congratulated him on a letter which was 'very nicely written' and had obviously been freely illustrated with caricatures. 'The sketches are from life I suppose. . . . Well, you have not made any of you very handsome.' As for one of the girls 'what a nose she has, and a cap fit for her grandmother'.

He entered the City of London School at the age of twelve, in September 1879. The school was then in Cheapside, and Arthur moved with it to the Victoria Embankment in 1883. Years later (28th June 1929) he wrote of his school days to his friend Howard Angus Kennedy, secretary of the Canadian Authors' Association:

'So we come from the same school! I went there first at the end of '79 so we were never together. Old Joey was still in great form, & was my master before the school moved to the Embankment – and a great master he was. Then at the "New School" – as we then called it, I settled down under Rushy, whose back benches I occupied for a long time – never flying higher. But he & I were friends until his death: & he had a great collection of my drawings – done in unorthodox hours & bagged by him. And even Abbott turned a blind eye to my delinquencies of that kind. . . .'

'Old Joey' was the Rev. Joseph Harris; 'Rushy' was W. G. Rushbrooke, the senior assistant classical master and a former Fellow of St John's College, Cambridge; and 'Abbott' was Edwin A. Abbott, the headmaster. Arthur did not distinguish himself particularly by his

scholarship, though he won several prizes, including one for mathematics in his last year; but he endeared himself to his masters by his humour and character, and by his precocious talent for drawing, which earned him the school prize (a portrait of himself by Herbert Dicksee, the drawing master, which seems not to have survived). His caricatures of the masters were so successful that he was asked to repeat one of Rushbrooke on the blackboard for the benefit of the whole form.

With all his high spirits, Arthur Rackham was a delicate boy, and at the end of 1883 Dr (later Sir) Samuel Wilks recommended that he should leave school and accompany two family friends, Miss Liggens and Mrs Merryfield, who were emigrating to Australia. Accordingly he sailed with them from Plymouth in the S.S. *Chimborazo* of the

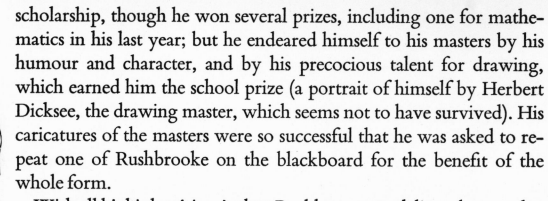

The five sketches of men in the margins are reproduced from original drawings in one of Rackham's scrap-books, and are dated 4 December 1892.

Orient Line on 26th January 1884, passing through the Mediterranean and the Suez Canal, and arriving at Sydney on 15th March. He spent about three months in Australia, returning in June in the S.S. *Iberia*. During the outward and homeward voyages, and during his stay in Australia, he painted many creditable water-colours. Vesuvius, Capri and the Suez Canal were among his subjects, but his *chef d'œuvre* was a 'Panoramic View of Sydney from Nature', dated May 1884. He arrived back in London in July with his health entirely re-established.

The long sea voyage, with its ample opportunities for sketching, had quite decided him to be an artist, and in the autumn of 1884 he entered the Lambeth School of Art. His fellow students included Leonard Raven-Hill, Thomas Sturge Moore, and Charles Ricketts; the last-named particularly influenced Rackham. But there was no question of his art-studies occupying the whole of his time; he had to prove his ability and work his way. Thus on 11th November 1884, his old masters Rushbrooke and Abbott both took up their pens on his behalf. Rushbrooke recommended him 'on the score of intelligence, industry and character', while his late headmaster Edwin Abbott declared that 'as regards ability, knowledge, character, and gentlemanly bearing Mr Arthur Rackham would be well suited for the clerkship he is now seeking in the Westminster Fire Office'.

Miss Nellie Stewart, the latest Comic Opera Debutante. *Pall Mall Budget*, 25 February 1892 (from a reproduction).

Sketch at the Palace Theatre   Mlle. Armand 'Ary. *Westminster Budget*, 24 February 1893 (from a reproduction).

CHAPTER TWO

Art School and After

THROUGHOUT the next seven years, from 1885 to 1892, Rackham sat on his stool in the insurance office and brought to his work there the methodical application and accurate accountancy which he showed in business affairs for the rest of his life. From his rooms in Buckingham Street he sent occasional contributions to the cheaper illustrated papers. His first crude published drawings had appeared in *Scraps* of 4th October 1884, illustrating the thesis: 'Mothers in Ceylon have a curious way of preventing their children from eating too much. A fine thread is tied round the child before it commences its meal, and when the thread breaks, the child is considered to have had enough.' Rackham demonstrated this with the minimum of subtlety. Another drawing, in *Scraps* of 15th November 1884, shows a little boy and a cat both trying to get their feet into their mouths, the cat with more success. His next drawing 'The Old Year and the New', published in *Illustrated Bits* of 3rd January 1885, was much more ambitious and attempted a light vein of prophecy, beginning with a piece of wishful thinking, the 'Triumphant Return of Wolseley and Gordon'. Rackham was already showing an interest in studies of animals; an egregious frog represented '1884 Leap Year', while lions and kangaroos played a test match Australia *v.* England. The next published work that he thought worth preserving was a fairly competent series of drawings of the City of London School's sports at Stamford Bridge in the *Daily Graphic* in the spring of 1890. But as early as 1887 he was painting water-colours of scenes near Leith Hill and on Wimbledon Common which, though academic and conventional, show an unusually fresh talent and fineness of execution. He painted many other promising water-colour landscapes in the south and west of England during his years in the Westminster Fire Office. A water-colour of Winchelsea was accepted by the Royal Academy in 1888, and sold for two guineas.

We are fortunate in having Rackham's own reminiscences and his considered opinion of this strenuous period in the office and the art school. They are contained in a letter to Mr W. E. Dawe, a young man who found himself in much the same dilemma as Rackham had done, and who wrote to ask Rackham's advice in 1909, when he was at the height of his fame. The letter is a remarkable example of disinterested generosity from a busy professional to an anxious beginner entirely unknown to him.

'16 Chalcot Gardens, South Hampstead, N.W.   23 August 09.

'Dear Mr Dawe,

'I was much interested by your letter and it will need rather a long letter to answer it satisfactorily. As you say you appear to be in much the same case as myself in having to go out into the world & earn your living at the age of 17; (and for the next seven years or so *I* worked as hard as I could out of business hours (9–5) to equip myself as an artist – not being able to embark on a professional career till I was nearly 25, & then for many years getting the barest living from my profession & having to do much distasteful hack work.)

'Now above all I do not want to be damping, but you must bear with my putting the case very plainly.

'To begin with at your age it is absolutely impossible to foretell what degree of talent you are gifted with. You are full of enthusiasm & feel good for anything – that's the best possible start but it will not be until you are much older & your art very fully developed technically that you can estimate your true powers.

'You say you send things to "Scraps", so did I at your age, though with the realisation of more serious artistic intentions I soon gave it up & devoted my time to the severest education. And that is the best advice I can give you.

'You might perhaps make a precarious living out of such work for Scraps &c – but after a few years of it, you would feel it cramping debasing hack work, killing the art in you, & robbing you of the joy of true art expression which is, after all, the one & only reason for your being an artist at all. The *living* from art is a poor one – for only a very few is it better. For numbers it is dismal failure – for some perhaps who appeared in youth to be really talented & who started with the utmost enthusiasm. And the outlook appears to get steadily worse. As a profession it is one to which no parent would be justified in putting a son without being able to give him a permanent income as well. Then, of course, if he fail, he will have something to live upon: I know several such, &, believe me, their bitter disappointment at their professional failure is only just prevented from being misery by the possession of an independent income.

'The fact that you can earn a little money at it now means very little. The standard of work that ensures a successful professional career is now technically very high and nothing but years of determined study can equip you for equal competition with the rest in the field.

'So this is my advice: – Stick to your business: go as regularly as you can with enthusiasm to a school of art (at New Cross, or Camberwell the schools are excellent) – among other things you will be associating & measuring yourself with the men who will be your

'The king could not contain himself for joy.' *The Fairy Tales of the Brothers Grimm;* a drawing of 1907.

professional companions later on & you will be able to estimate your relative powers – (remembering that if 2 or 3 in the school at any one time are ever heard of as artists in 10 or 20 years time, it is about as much as you can expect). And without a full, *general* art education you can hardly tell yet in what line you are likely to succeed. For the rest, you must keep yourself fit. You say you find it a strain – well you must do the best you can by sharing your spare time between art study & exercise & other recreations. I myself used to chafe at being able to give comparatively so little time to it while my companions were giving their whole time. But for your comfort I may say that I believe the brain goes on developing on artistic lines in an enthusiastic nature almost as quickly in spite of the shorter time given to actual performance.

'Then in 5 or 6 years you may find that your proved ability justifies you in joining the ranks of professional artists. And if, as is within the bounds of possibility, it doesn't, you will be far happier living by your business, and practising art as an enthusiastic amateur than as a disappointed, pot-boiling professional.

'Is this a very disappointing letter? – you needn't regard it so – for whether you are a genius or not there is only one way of discovering it – it can't be done without years of study – in art as in any other profession (only perhaps more in art than in any other profession). If you have ability, in 10 years you'll have shewn it, & you will be, professionally, a mere youth with the future before you. And you will not have burnt your boats too soon.

'So stick to your business for the present.

'Go to the best school of art in your neighbourhood, enjoy your art education, the competition of the schools. Don't waste time attempting to earn money at it now, it's not worth it. Wait till you can go into the arena properly trained. Carry a sketch book – at least I did & have never regretted the assiduous thoughtful sketching I did. It is the most splendid training for brain, hand, & eye.

'They worked themselves up into such a rage that they tore up trees by the roots . . .'
The Fairy Tales of the Brothers Grimm; a drawing of 1906.

Becket at Windsor. *Westminster Budget*, 24 March 1893.

35

'Show your people this letter & talk it over with them & you have my very best wishes for your happiness & success in my profession.

'Believe me

Sincerely yours

Arthur Rackham'

In the event, Mr Dawe stayed in the City, and he has not regretted that he remained an amateur. 'Now in retirement I have the more time to practise the art I've never ceased to love,' he wrote in 1958. 'That it has worked out like this would have pleased Rackham.'

With Rackham, of course, it was otherwise. Throughout 1891 his work proved increasingly acceptable to the *Pall Mall Budget*. In 1891 and 1892 there were few weeks in which his drawing was not represented in that paper. We may follow through his eyes the day-to-day life of London, most diligently recorded. He sketched in the shops and in the streets of London, in the railway stations, at the theatres, in the churches, at the Zoo, and at Burlington House on 'sending-in day'. He was ready to make excursions to the country or the seaside, and in July 1891, his drawings of 'A Little Holiday in Belgium' with his friend Walter Freeman filled two pages of the *P.M.B.* The humours of cockney cabmen or 'Winter Bathing in the Serpentine' alternated with funeral tributes to the Duke of Clarence or C. H. Spurgeon.

'Sketches from the Life' of public personalities became one of his specialities, and these appeared more frequently after he left the insurance office in 1892 and joined the staff of the *Westminster Budget*. His work, prominently featured in the first number of the new paper (2nd February 1893), was published regularly in its pages for the next three years. The larger format of the *Westminster Budget* gave him new scope; his drawings of well-known contemporaries became a popular feature, and in retrospect form a remarkable record of life in the 'nineties. Ready to go anywhere and do

The influenza fiend. *W.B.*, 22 December 1893.

More interesting than any of these early efforts were Rackham's four halftone illustrations and cover design for the first edition in book form of *The Dolly Dialogues* by Anthony Hope (1894) which had originally appeared without illustrations in the *Westminster Gazette*. These drawings, stilted as they were – the cover design (see page 41) is the best of them, being in the Beggarstaff manner – served to link Rackham's name for the first time with a work of literary merit. Soon afterwards came drawings for Washington Irving's *The Sketchbook of Geoffrey Crayon, Gent.* (1894), *Tales of a Traveller* (1895), and *Bracebridge Hall* (1896); illustrations in *Little Folks* (1896) for a story by his friend Maggie Browne; charming work for Fanny Burney's *Evelina* (1898); capable designs for various gardening and nature books; and conventional romanticism for cloak-and-dagger novels by H. S. Merriman and Stanley Weyman.

Rackham's work in the 'nineties displayed versatility and experiment. The journalist predominated, it is true, with his large output of factual reportage of high quality. But at the same time a remarkable draughtsman was developing; his pencil studies of old men, dated 1895, in Mrs Harris Rackham's collection, show him to have learned from Charles Keene (see page 47). Beardsley had become another considerable influence (Rackham parodied Beardsley engagingly in the *Westminster Budget* of 20th July 1894, but Beardsley was nonetheless a serious influence on his style), and with him the whole German school from Dürer to Menzel and Hans Thoma. The fanciful and poetic element gradually supplanted the conventional as Rackham's technique developed.

Before the 'nineties were out, Rackham had to his credit, besides many drawings for *Cassell's Magazine*, *Little Folks* and other papers, the illustrations for two books published by J. M. Dent which were to prove more important to his career than anything he had hitherto produced. These were *The Ingoldsby Legends* of 1898 (see page 23) and Charles and Mary Lamb's *Tales from Shakespeare* (1899).

anything for his paper, Rackham portrayed many of the leading actresses, sportsmen, writers, and politicians of the day. The Queen and Mr Gladstone were among his most frequent subjects. He was often called upon to celebrate royal occasions (see pages 35 and 37).

Some of Rackham's voluminous journalism is shown in this book. For the most part it is conventional and unimaginative – in striking contrast to the work by which he is best known – but already he was demonstrating his mastery of line. An artist so deft and conscientious was an asset to the *Westminster Budget*. And there were moments, as with his disquieting full-page fantasy 'The Influenza Fiend' (1893), which unmistakably foreshadowed the fanciful and at times weirdly imaginative illustrator that he was to become.

Rackham continued to draw for the *Westminster Budget* until 1896 but from 1893 onwards became increasingly occupied with book illustrations. His first published book (1893) was a *Norddeutscher Lloyd* travel brochure, *To The Other Side* by Thomas Rhodes, now very scarce, for which he provided black-and-white drawings in the careful rounded style of his early water-colours. The drawings included views of Salt Lake City and San Francisco; of the Sentinel Rock, Yosemite, the Royal Gorge and Pike's Peak, all based on photographs. Ten of these drawings fetched eighty pounds when they were sold at Sothebys in 1957. Other commercial commissions were for an illustrated guide to Wells-next-the-Sea (1894) and for seventy-five drawings in *Sunrise-Land: Rambles in Eastern England* by Mrs Alfred Berlyn (1894), both books carrying advertisements for the Great Eastern Railway. Some of his journalistic work also reappeared in book form, notably a full page drawing of Irving from the *Westminster Budget* which was included in Walter Calvert's *Souvenir of Sir Henry Irving* (1895), while one of his drawings of Gladstone was used to illustrate *In the Evening of his Days: A Study of Mr Gladstone in Retirement* by Hulda Friederichs (1896).

'With this ring I thee wed': The Duke puts on the ring. *Westminster Budget*, 7 July 1893 (from a reproduction).

The Patient. *Westminster Budget*, 15 June 1894 (from a reproduction).

Neither of these books can be favourably compared with the best of Rackham's later work, but they show him at an interesting phase of his development. The fiend who blows the horn in 'The Lay of St Cuthbert's; or The Devil's Dinner-Party' in *Ingoldsby* is recognizably the same fellow as 'The Influenza Fiend' of 1893 and the Caliban from the Lambs' *Tales* of 1899, but in his mere ugliness he is a crude precursor of later devils. The artist's ever-increasing popularity during the next decade led to the publisher's decision to re-issue *Ingoldsby* and the *Tales from Shakespeare*, in 1907 and 1909 respectively, with additional illustrations. In some respects this was regrettable. Rackham provided admirable new frontispieces for both books and worked on many of the old colour plates. The 1907 *Ingoldsby*, in its vellum-bound limited edition, is valued by collectors, but the book as a whole lacks consistency of vision. Authentic Rackham is to be found in the frontispiece and occasionally elsewhere, but might seem to have been imposed on a medley borrowed from Beardsley, Hugh Thomson and the monkish slapstick of John Hassall. By 1907 Rackham had not only outdistanced his own earlier self but had also outgrown the coarse humours of Barham.

When Rackham was asked by *The Bookman* (October 1925) to contribute to a symposium on 'The Worst Time in My Life', he said that for several years at the beginning of his career he had had 'far from an easy time', but added that the Boer War 'was a very thin time indeed for me, and may be considered the worst time I have ever had'. Rackham had little liking or aptitude for the sort of journalistic work then in demand; he realized, moreover, that the camera would soon largely supplant the artist in illustrated journalism. His financial success as an illustrator, though merited and overdue, was also a matter of practical necessity.

Title-page sketches for *The Vicar of Wakefield*.

Cover design for the first edition of *The Dolly Dialogues*.

CHAPTER THREE

Marriage and Success

ALTHOUGH by the end of the century Rackham had made his mark as an illustrator, and although the responsibilities of marriage which he assumed soon afterwards increased his determination to devote himself to this branch of his art, there are some early sketches in oils, including a self-portrait of 1892 (see page 55), which show that he was anxious to experiment in that medium, while several interesting and highly deliberate portraits and self-portraits, undertaken at intervals throughout his life, emphasize that portraiture remained one of his unfulfilled ambitions. It is probable that he was never fully satisfied with his portraits and doubted his ability to make a livelihood out of them, with the result – which we cannot regret – that he devoted himself to that kind of work, mostly based on themes provided by literature, which the public came to expect of him and in which he was successful both financially and artistically. But it would be a mistake to suppose that as a young man he was untouched by the appeal of impressionism, for example, or that he fell into his career as an illustrator without any searching of his artistic conscience. In particular, he was well aware that by concentrating on illustration he was limiting his objectives and would be likely to take rank, save for the discriminating few, as a 'minor artist'.

To his work in his chosen field Rackham brought the gifts of an unusual visual memory, especially for landscape and natural growth in all its forms (less, perhaps, for architecture), and a fertile imagination guiding a hand of great sensibility and skill in draughtsmanship. He was fond of children and a close observer of their moods and movements; he understood the delight most of them have in fairies, which does not mean that he himself 'believed in fairies'. He had also a keen eye for the odd and grotesque and for the ironies of incongruous juxtaposition.

Some of his drawings – those for Edgar Allan Poe, for example – could be gruesome, and there was 'symbolism', conscious or unconscious, in many of the fairy tales he illustrated. But an analysis of 'symbolism' in Rackham's drawings, or a psychological interpretation of his work – not many of his commissions, be it remembered, were entirely of his own choosing – would be unlikely to reveal interesting repressions or afford valuable insights into Rackham's character. Gifted with a prolific poetic imagination and fertile invention, he enjoyed a cheerful happy temperament. Methodical and businesslike, he was careful with his money but could be exceedingly generous in presents to others.

If Rackham depended for general inspiration on the pre-Raphaelite tradition and on the Gothic and Italian primitives, more particular influences on his style may be found in Cruikshank, Caldecott, Dicky Doyle, Arthur Boyd Houghton, the artists of Germany and Japan, and the decorative contrasts of Beardsley. There was in Rackham's work, as in that of Charles Ricketts, his contemporary at the Lambeth School of Art, a flavour of Art Nouveau, which is especially noticeable in some of his cover designs and borders of illustrations, and in the elaborate curves of his foam-topped waves. But this influence, never predominant, was a diminishing one before 1914. By contrast

A nightmare: horrible result of contemplating an Aubrey Beardsley after supper. *W.B.*, 20 July 1894.

he was an admirer of the work of Edmund J. Sullivan and helped him from his earnings as early as 1900 ('My dear Rackham, you're a brick,' reads one of Sullivan's letters to him in that year). When it was suggested that he might have been influenced by Indian miniatures, Rackham wrote to his brother Bernard (22nd September 1936):

'I was amazed at the comparison of my work with the Indian. Except in one or two later drawings there has been no direct or even suspected influence. Actually, but remotely, more from the Japanese. But of course my very general use of the bounding line is a usual oriental style. I think I myself am more conscious of Teutonic influence. . . . Thinking it over, I fancy the only drawings I have done consciously influenced by the Indian are one (only one I think) in The Tempest, and two (especially The Old Man of the Sea) in The Rackham Fairy Book. P.S. And, when consciously, it has been Persian rather than Indian.'

The first year of the new century marked a turning point in Rackham's career, for in it were published his original illustrations for *Fairy Tales of the Brothers Grimm* (see pages 31 and 33) – ninety-nine drawings in black and white with a coloured frontispiece. The book was immediately successful, and its publication marked the beginning of Rackham's lasting fame. Two new editions were called for within ten years. At intervals from 1900 onwards Rackham worked on the original drawings, partially or entirely redrawing some of them in colour, adding new ones in colour and in black-and-white, and generally overhauling them as a set, until the final and best-known edition, of 1909, contained forty coloured illustrations and fifty-five line drawings. Rackham wrote to Frank Redway on 28th May 1914: 'In many ways I have more affection for the Grimm drawings than for other sets. (I think it is partly one's childhood affection for the stories.) It was the first book I did that began to bring success (the little, earlier edition, that is). . . .'

In this letter Rackham touches on one important reason for his triumph as an illustrator of the classics – his very thorough knowledge of the texts. Though he was completely faithful to his authors, there was nothing of slavish pedantry in his interpretations; the personal and imaginative always transcended the literal. A comparison between the first and the last editions of his *Grimm* emphasizes the remarkable progress that Rackham made in a decade; yet the earlier drawings that he allowed to stand can hold their own with the later ones. A reviewer of the enlarged book in the *Westminster Gazette* of 1909 enlisted the help of two small boys to make another point that

Madame Zola at the
Mansion House. *W.B.,*
29 September 1893.

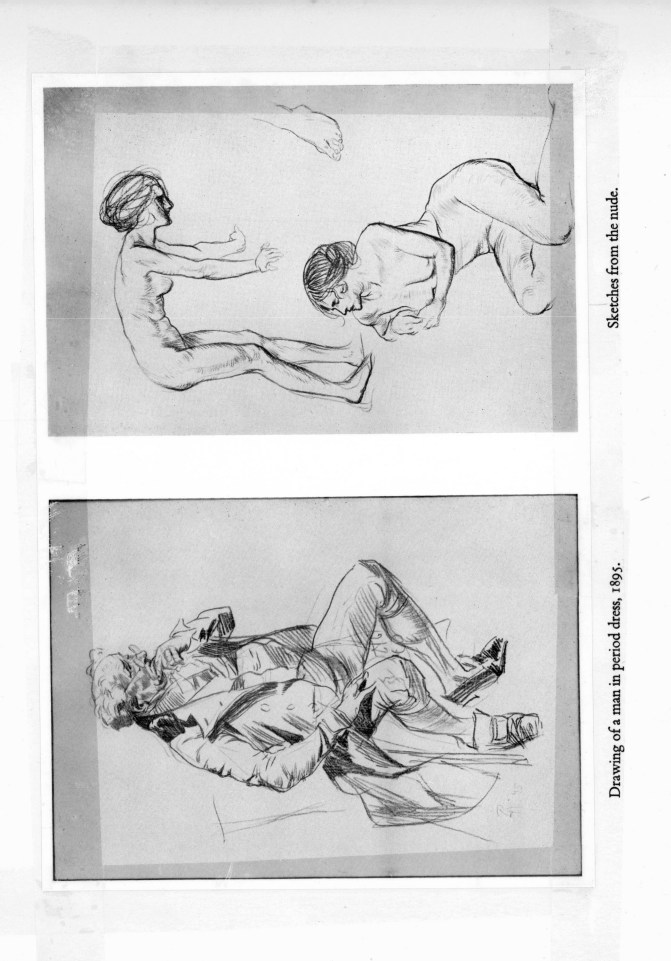

Sketches from the nude.

Drawing of a man in period dress, 1895.

told strikingly in Rackham's favour: 'When it came to the contemplation of Mr Rackham's drawings there was never a second's hesitation. They understood them at once, and entirely.'

Nevertheless, even after 1900, the fanciful element in Rackham, where his true genius lay, did not overcome the temptations of the commercial or conventional without a struggle. During the next few years he contributed many drawings to the sporting and 'open-air' books in Dent's Haddon Hall Library; he also illustrated such diverse publications as *Mysteries of Police and Crime* (1901) which he had anticipated in drawings for a magazine article several years earlier, Dana's *Two Years Before the Mast* (1904), and *Gulliver's Travels*, for an edition that was refurbished, like his *Grimm*, when his reputation had advanced. He was particularly successful with his dramatic contrasts in *Gulliver*. All this was but a part of a very large miscellaneous output.

He received strong encouragement to follow his natural bent for fantasy from his fellow artist and future wife Edyth Starkie, whom he met about the year 1900 when she and her mother were neighbours of his in Wychcomb Studios, Englands Lane, Hampstead. Her nephew Walter Starkie's earliest memories of Rackham date from that year. Walter had arrived from Dublin, aged six, on a visit to his grandmother. 'My first impression of the painter was coloured by the fairy stories my aunt Edyth told me at bedtime,' he writes. 'His face was wizened and wrinkled like a ripe walnut, and as he peered short-sightedly at me out of his goggle spectacles I thought he was one of the goblins out of Grimm's Fairy Tales. Dressed in his shabby blue suit and hopping about his studio in his carpet slippers, he reminded me of Rumpelstiltskin, but when he was armed with palette and paint brushes he became for me a wizard, who with one touch of his magic wand could people my universe with elves and leprechauns. He would take me out for walks over Primrose Hill or in Kensington Gardens where he would sketch the trees, and as he worked he would

How authors work: Mr Hall Caine – the clock strikes five! *Westminster Budget*, 5 October 1894 (from a reproduction).

Richardson, the crack Surrey Bowler. *Westminster Budget*, 9 June 1893 (from a reproduction).

G

After the ball. *W.B.*, 20 October 1893.

tell me stories of gnomes who lived in the roots and churned butter out of the sap flowing from the knotted branches.'

This may have been an exaggerated view of Rackham at the age of thirty-three, but it is true to say that in appearance he had aged rapidly – his, after all, was a life of intense application. The clear-cut, earnest, distinguished features above the high collar (as we see them in many early photographs) soon became deeply grooved; he lost his hair young; except in bed, he was never without steel or gold-rimmed spectacles, of which he owned a great variety – reading spectacles, spectacles for tennis, bi-focal spectacles. He remained a neat, alert person, tidy, energetic, punctual. Amateur theatricals were for many years a persistent interest; in 1900 he played Blore the butler in Pinero's *Dandy Dick*, and he also designed the scenery and acted in performances of Gilbert and Sullivan. He kept himself fit with lawn tennis and exercise on a trapeze. He was active and precise in all he did, whether working or playing, in which there was really little difference since he enjoyed his work and took his play seriously. If he grew slightly balder, more wrinkled and silvery during the years, this hardly altered his general appearance.

Edyth Starkie, with a smooth pink-and-white complexion, un-lined to the end of her life, with wide-open Irish blue eyes ever full of mischief, her hair snow-white from an early age, was the antithesis of Arthur Rackham in character. She had a charm which made everybody like her and many people love her. If she was not convention-ally beautiful, she gave the impression of beauty. She made her friends laugh without ever really saying anything particularly witty, and she could give great comfort by her sympathy and understand-ing. Servants and tradesmen adored her. An original experimenter in interior decoration, she was keen on new ideas of all kinds, with a passion for motoring and later for the wireless. She would launch herself into daring arguments in favour of free-love or Communism – but entirely theoretically, for she herself lived the mildest and

Two photographs of Arthur Rackham at his drawing board, one taken in his thirties, the other in later life.

strictest of lives. 'I rather like bad people but I can't stand bad art' – that phrase has seemed to her daughter to sum up exactly her attitude to life.

By the time that she met Arthur Rackham, who was two months older than herself, Edyth Starkie already knew much of the world. Born on the west coast of Ireland at Westcliff, near Galway, on 27th November 1867, the youngest of six, she had spent most of her youth at Cregane Manor, Rosscarbery, near Cork, a curious mixture of a house, basically old but with considerable Victorian additions, standing stark on a headland overlooking Rosscarbery Bay. Its white-washed walls, Gothic doorways, and castellations, and its jumble of soft blue-grey slate roofs, are ringed round by a grove of windswept trees; dotted about the grounds are the whitewashed cottages of 'the tenants'. There Edyth rode to hounds, sailed in the bay and teased her brothers' tutors. Her father, R. M. Starkie, apparently an attractive but lazy man, is said to have performed his duties as Resident Magistrate in dilatory fashion, but taught himself to play the violin, an accomplishment inherited by his grandson Walter.

When Edyth was sixteen, her mother took her on a tour of Europe. They stayed for a time in Paris, where Edyth studied art, and then went on to Germany, where she became engaged to a Prussian officer at Potsdam, causing a major scandal when she broke off the engagement. After her father's death, she settled in Hampstead with her mother.

Arthur Rackham admired her not only as a woman but also as an artist, who was then achieving a considerable reputation as a portrait painter. Her pictures are intensely individual and sincere. They are remarkable for their deep sense of character, and with their low tones and sombre lighting recall the early portraits of James Pryde. Like Pryde, she was a member of the International Society; works by her were bought for the National Museum, Barcelona, where she won a gold medal in 1911, and the Luxembourg, Paris.

Arthur Rackham: a self-portrait in oils, aged 24.

Edyth Starkie: a self-portrait in oils, probably aged about 20.

Although her career was broken by ill-health, she was an artist to be remembered with honour.

It will be readily understood, then, how much Rackham owed to his wife, who was married to him at St Mark's, Hampstead, on 16th July 1903 (she was a lapsed Catholic, the Rackham family were Anglicans turned Unitarians). His alliance with this gay artistic Irishwoman brought out the best in Rackham; for she was always his most stimulating, severest critic, and he had the greatest respect for her opinion. In return he gave her unswerving loyalty and devotion, so that the marriage, despite its temperamental ups-and-downs, proved a very happy one. Walter Starkie shows the nature of it:

'Aunt Edyth was the romantic one of the family, and my father used to tell my sister Enid and myself anecdotes of her flirtations and her seven engagements, and the story of the duels that had been fought for her when she was an art student in Germany. My uncle was taciturn and observant, and would cock his head and look at my aunt quizzically when my father used to embroider these stories. Uncle Arthur had a strange habit of disappearing and re-appearing suddenly like the Cat in *Alice in Wonderland*. When my aunt would say: "I wonder where Arthur is," he would appear a moment later by her side as though he had popped up through a trap door. He was more staid than my aunt, and with his prim precise English manner was an admirable foil and when in company she would always do her best to shock him.'

Rackham had exhibited successfully at the Royal Academy, at the Institute of Painters in Water-Colours, at a 'Loan Exhibition of Modern Illustration' at South Kensington (1901), and at various provincial exhibitions before he was elected an Associate of The Royal Water-Colour Society in February 1902 (he became a full member in

Edyth Starkie: a self-portrait in oils, probably aged about 20.

Arthur Rackham: a self-portrait in oils, aged 24.

MARRIAGE AND SUCCESS

Although her career was broken by ill-health, she was an artist to be remembered with honour.

It will be readily understood, then, how much Rackham owed to his wife, who was married to him at St Mark's, Hampstead, on 16th July 1903 (she was a lapsed Catholic, the Rackham family were Anglicans turned Unitarians). His alliance with this gay artistic Irishwoman brought out the best in Rackham; for she was always his most stimulating, severest critic, and he had the greatest respect for her opinion. In return he gave her unswerving loyalty and devotion, so that the marriage, despite its temperamental ups-and-downs, proved a very happy one. Walter Starkie shows the nature of it:

'Aunt Edyth was the romantic one of the family, and my father used to tell my sister Enid and myself anecdotes of her flirtations and her seven engagements, and the story of the duels that had been fought for her when she was an art student in Germany. My uncle was taciturn and observant, and would cock his head and look at my aunt quizzically when my father used to embroider these stories. Uncle Arthur had a strange habit of disappearing and re-appearing suddenly like the Cat in *Alice in Wonderland*. When my aunt would say: "I wonder where Arthur is," he would appear a moment later by her side as though he had popped up through a trap door. He was more staid than my aunt, and with his prim precise English manner was an admirable foil and when in company she would always do her best to shock him.'

Rackham had exhibited successfully at the Royal Academy, at the Institute of Painters in Water-Colours, at a 'Loan Exhibition of Modern Illustration' at South Kensington (1901), and at various provincial exhibitions before he was elected an Associate of The Royal Water-Colour Society in February 1902 (he became a full member in

1908). He received considerable encouragement to pursue his individual style of decorative illustration from the Friday evening meetings of the Langham Sketching Club, of which he was chairman for two consecutive years, 1905–6 and 1906–7 – a sure proof of his popularity with his fellow artists, for the chairman was elected primarily to preside at the supper table. His 'Windfalls', now in the Melbourne National Gallery, and 'Cupid's Alley', now in the Tate Gallery (see page 59), were both painted in 1904; 'The Magic Carpet' was bought for the Bradford Gallery in 1907 and 'Treasures of the Deep' for the Preston Gallery in 1909. But the first work that greatly advanced his fame in the years immediately following his marriage was his edition of *Rip Van Winkle*, with its fifty-one colour plates, published in 1905.

This lovely book decisively established Rackham as the leading decorative illustrator of the Edwardian period. One does not know which to admire most – the superb artistry of his landscapes, the poetry of the scenes of Rip by the riverside, the charm of his children and fairies, or the grotesque groups of Henrick Hudson and his crew which so long anticipated the art of Walt Disney (see pages 63 and 65). With *Rip Van Winkle* he began his fruitful association with the firm of William Heinemann, who issued the book in a limited edition and a trade edition, while American, French, German and other foreign editions were also called for, setting a pattern of publication to be followed for many years. Another profitable precedent was established by the exhibition of the originals at the Leicester Galleries in March 1905. All except eight of the pictures were sold, and the *deluxe* edition of the book was fully subscribed before the exhibition closed. Henceforth Rackham's book illustrations were regularly exhibited at the Leicester Galleries at the time of their publication, and they found ready buyers.

E. V. Lucas was one of those who wrote to him at this time:

'2 Gordon Place, Campden Hill, W.   March 29, 1905

'Dear Mr Rackham,

'I have at last been able to get to your exhibition; which I enjoyed immensely. Hitherto one has had to go to the Continent for so much mingled grace & grotesque as you have given us. The drawings seem to me extraordinarily successful & charming. The only thing I quarrel with is the prevalence of "sold" tickets – one on every picture that I liked best. Barrie tells me he has the same grievance. I am glad to hear that you think of treating Peter Pan in the same vein. Believe me yours sincerely,

E. V. Lucas'

Invitation card, printed in sepia, 11 March 1905.

The Dance in Cupid's Alley. A drawing of 1904 illustrating Austin Dobson's lines: 'O, Love's but a dance, where Time plays the fiddle!' (Tate Gallery).

Rackham had begun to draw for *Punch* in the Almanac at Christmas 1904, and another who now congratulated him on 'a very successful show' was F. C. Burnand, the editor. 'If you have anything that might suit Punch,' Burnand urged on 7th April 1905, 'will you let me see it – or *them*? Whether singular or plural the drawings shall be returned directly I have seen them if they are not quite what we require in Punch and I may be then able to suggest some "legends" you might like to treat for Mr Punch's gallery.'

Henceforth Rackham was an occasional contributor to *Punch* whenever his commitments allowed. We see him thus in 1905 at the outset of twenty years of the most prolific and prosperous creative work ever enjoyed by an English illustrator.

CHAPTER FOUR

Peter Pan and Alice

UCAS had hinted, in his letter of March 1905, congratulating Rackham on the *Rip Van Winkle* exhibition, at J. M. Barrie's interest in his work and at the prospect of his undertaking illustrations for *Peter Pan*. It was not intended that he should illustrate the famous play, successfully produced for the first time the previous Christmas and not published until 1928, but rather those chapters from that rambling book *The Little White Bird* (1902) which had introduced Peter Pan to the world, though in a form very different from that in which he is seen on the stage. Rackham could have found no subject more immediately topical, or more fashionably propitious. *Peter Pan in Kensington Gardens*, as he re-created it, and as it appeared from Hodder and Stoughton with fifty full-page illustrations in colour mounted on thick paper according to the taste of the time (see pages 67, 69, 73, 75), became the outstanding Christmas gift-book of 1906 – and maintained its hold for many later Christmases. The pattern of publication continued as before, with a limited edition, a trade edition, an American edition, and a French edition (1907) of *Piter Pan: Les Jardins de Kensington*.

The initiative in commissioning these drawings came from Messrs

Ernest Brown and Phillips of the Leicester Galleries, who arranged a meeting between Rackham and Barrie for a preliminary discussion in June 1905:

'Black Lake Cottage, Nr. Farnham, Surrey.   11 June 1905.

'Dear Mr Rackham,
    'Let us say about five o'clock on Thursday as that day suits you. I shall expect you then at Leinster Corner, which is the first house past Lancaster Gate in the Bayswater Rd. It's round the corner.
                                        'Yours sincerely,
                                            J. M. Barrie'

Rackham worked steadily on the book for the next year, making many sketches in Kensington Gardens, and then wrote to propose another meeting at which he could show the author his finished pictures. He found Barrie pre-occupied by the illness of his friend Arthur Llewelyn Davies:

'Leinster Corner, Lancaster Gate, W.   18 June, 1906.

'Dear Mr Rackham,
    'I am so much at present with a friend who is dangerously ill that I have not seen my letters till now, so kindly excuse this delay in answering. I want so much to see the pictures, and thank you heartily for your letter. Could you come on Wednesday about six o'clock? I shall be here if this suits you.
                                        'Yours sincerely,
                                            J. M. Barrie'

A few months later he gave Rackham some last-minute advice about

'He would sit on a wet rock and fish all day.' *Rip Van Winkle*, 1905:
a drawing of 1904.

the map of Kensington Gardens which appeared on the front end-paper:

'Leinster Corner, Lancaster Gate, W.   22 Oct. 1906

'Dear Mr Rackham,
    'The sheep shearing nowadays is done where I put the cross (be-hind the cottage at that point.) Fairies Basin south of Baby Walk.
    'I haven't seen a dummy book but H. & S. sent me some speci-men pictures which I liked hugely.
                                    'Yours sincerely,
                                        J. M. Barrie'

In the next two letters Barrie referred to the exhibition of Rackham's *Peter Pan* pictures at the Leicester Galleries:

'Leinster Corner, Lancaster Gate, W.   16 Nov.

'Dear Mr Rackham,
    'Unfortunately I am going out of town Saty till Monday, other-wise I shd have accepted your invitation with much pleasure. How-ever I have accepted a proposal from the Gallery to go in & see the pictures before the opening day. May it all be a great triumph for you.
                                    'Yours sincerely,
                                        J. M. Barrie'

'Leinster Corner, Lancaster Gate, W.   18 Dec. 1906

'My dear Rackham,
    'It was immensely good of you to put that delicious little picture in my copy of "Peter". I have been a wreck with colds & coughs for

'A company of odd-looking persons playing at ninepins.' *Rip Van Winkle*: a drawing of 1904.

I

six weeks which is why I have not written you sooner, especially about the exhibition. It entranced me. I think I like best of all the Serpentine with the fairies, and the Peter in his night-gown sitting in the tree. Next I would [*sic*] the flying Peters, the fairies going to the ball (as in the "tiff" & the fairy on cobweb) – the fairies sewing the leaves with their sense of fun (the gayest thing this) and your treatment of snow. I am always your debtor, and I wish the happiest Christmas, and please, I hope you will shed glory on more of my things.

'Yours most sincerely,
J. M. Barrie'

The critics were largely of Barrie's view in the matter, as, for example, the *Pall Mall Gazette*: 'Not the least part of that good fortune that follows Mr Barrie's steps is his choice of an illustrator. Mr Rackham seems to have dropped out of some cloud in Mr Barrie's fairyland, sent by a special providence to make pictures in tune to his whimsical genius.' Rackham's friends and fellow illustrators were genuinely delighted at his success. 'It may be that your pictures are a craze, that people have lost their heads and that the dealers are keeping the thing up – it may be!' wrote Harry Rountree. 'All I know is that I am as intoxicated as the worst and I am certain that this drunkenness will last for ever. . . . Long live Rackham!' At the same time, it is only fair to mention that there were one or two critics who were more doubtful, who sneered at these 'children's books' that were designed for the drawing-room rather than the nursery (probably true, though they were appreciated in both quarters), and who obscurely resented the luxurious pages, the tissue fly-leaves, the 'fluttering prints each half-mounted on a sheet of brown paper in approved collector-fashion'. They would have agreed with David Bland in *The Illustration of Books* (1951) that for all Rackham's skill in using the three-colour (or four-colour) process and drawing for it with pen and

'Old Mr Salford was a crab-apple of an old gentleman who wandered all day in the
Gardens.' *Peter Pan in Kensington Gardens*, 1906
(by courtesy of Hodder and Stoughton Ltd).

water-colour – the care that he took to achieve faithful colour reproduction was extraordinary – his Edwardian books were 'more distinguished by their opulent appearance than by any bookish quality'. This criticism cannot be brought to bear on the exquisite black-and-white work with which Rackham decorated the text pages of these and later books. If there is some truth in it, the fault lay not with Rackham but with the fashion of the time. His achievement in the contemporary convention of illustration was a superb one; and the collectors' demand for his books, here and in America, has shown it to be lasting.

The *Peter Pan* book was a landmark in the life of Rackham's nephew, Walter Starkie, who writes of it:

'Whereas Rackham's illustrations of Washington Irving's tale fascinated me by their quaint touches of Dutch-American realism in contrast with the eerie atmosphere of the mountains and the ghostly figures playing bowls, *Peter Pan* became the consecration of my childhood, for I had watched my uncle's sensitive and agile paint-brushes people those trees with dwarfs and gnomes, and he had often drawn the children's map of Kensington Gardens before taking me on the Grand Tour through what Sir James Barrie called "the pleasantest club in London". Although we children went again and again to the theatre to see the play, it was through the Rackham illustrations of Kensington Gardens and the Serpentine that Peter Pan still lived in our memories. (At school, however, Gentleman Starkie became my "bête noire", for I was forever known as "miserable Starkie"). Years afterwards my uncle introduced me to Sir James Barrie after a performance of *Dear Brutus* and it was the beautiful actress Faith Celli's inspired acting that brought back all my childhood memories of those illustrations, for Faith Celli was the embodiment of the Arthur Rackham heroine.'

'The Serpentine is a lovely lake, and there is a drowned forest at the bottom of
it.' *Peter Pan in Kensington Gardens* (by courtesy of
Hodder and Stoughton Ltd).

The Rackhams' first joint home was at 3, Primrose Hill Studios, Fitzroy Road (near Primrose Hill), but he was soon able to move to an attractive, unusual, high-gabled house at 16, Chalcot Gardens, Englands Lane, which had been built in 1881 and enlarged in 1898 by W. Voysey. The back of the house was mostly taken up by two large studios, one used by Mrs Rackham, and the other (which Maxwell Ayrton added for him) by Rackham himself. From this upper studio a spiral staircase ran down into the peaceful garden with its trees. The studio was full of curiosities, and for many years it usually contained a large Persian tabby-cat, called 'Sir James' after Barrie, who would put a stop to all work when he brought his comb to be groomed every afternoon. 'There is nothing disappointing about the little house in Chalcot Gardens,' wrote Eleanor Farjeon in an article. 'Out-wardly it is not unsuited to the pages of fairy tale. It has a mellow red-and-brown charm, and is the kind of house that could very well have been built of gingerbread and candy. Behind the house is the kind of garden that makes me feel six years old again. . . .'

When he married, Rackham was earning considerably less than a thousand pounds annually, but he soon reached and passed that figure, and from 1907 onwards his earned income fluctuated for many years between £1,500 and £3,500. In one remarkable year (1920) he earned £7,000. He soon found that he could rely on heavy royalties from his books, and also that he could sell his originals at good prices, especially if they were in colour (it proved worth while for him to add colour to his black-and-white drawings for this purpose). He was able to save and he invested his savings carefully; while his steady support of the Artists' General Benevolent Institution showed that he was always mindful of those less fortunate than himself.

Rackham's next undertaking after *Peter Pan* was the most contro-versial of his whole career. This was nothing less than a fresh illustra-tion of *Alice in Wonderland*, a work so completely identified with the drawings by John Tenniel that it seemed to many critics almost

Above, the house at 16 Chalcot Gardens, Hampstead, with Rackham on a balcony: a photograph taken in autumn 1913. Below, Houghton House, near Arundel; Rackham's studio is on the left of the picture.

blasphemous for anyone to attempt to prepare alternatives. As soon as it became clear, however, that a spate of new illustrated editions was being planned to follow the expiry of the original copyright (in fact, at least seven appeared in England in the first possible year, 1907), it was surely not to be regretted that an artist of Rackham's quality had taken up the challenge. Even *The Times*, in the course of an unfavourable review, recognized that Rackham 'feels his privilege and his responsibilities', but this critic, obsessed by Tenniel, found Rackham's humour 'forced and derivative' and discovered 'few signs of true imaginative instinct' in his work. A stranger wrote at once to sympathize: 'I felt I *must* express my indignation at the injustice of the "Times" criticism. However, I am certain that Time is on your side, and that nothing but prejudice prevents your superiority being recognised now. Your delightful Alice is alive and makes by contrast Tenniel's Alice look a stiff wooden puppet.'

'I'll fetch you ladies a chair apiece'
... The quintessence of all
charwomanhood. *W.B.*, 1894.

' "Preposterous!" cried Solomon in a rage.' *Peter Pan in Kensington Gardens* (by courtesy of Hodder and Stoughton Ltd).

PETER PAN AND ALICE

This went much further than Rackham would have done, for he
had no wish to set himself up against Tenniel. He would have been
well content with the verdict of the *Daily Telegraph*, that it would be
fortunate for Lewis Carroll's memory if his masterpiece encountered
'no less inspired interpreters than Mr Arthur Rackham'. When *Punch*
published a hostile cartoon by E. T. Reed, another illustrator, H. M.
Brock, told Rackham that he was 'disgusted'.

'It seems to me like a piece of exceedingly bad taste, to say nothing
of its unfairness. . . . Of course, you were prepared for everyone to
say that no one could ever approach Tenniel etc. – they always do in
such a case – but it seems to me that if comparisons – always "odor-
ous" – must be drawn, they might be done decently. I should like
too, to say how much I personally like your drawings. I would not
have missed them in spite of all that Tenniel has had to say on the
subject. . . .'

Brock's opinion coincided with the general verdict on Rackham's
Alice. He has certainly made the greatest impression of all Tenniel's
multitude of successors. The Rackham volume is still in print with
Heinemann (1960) and the illustrations have appeared in American,
French and German editions (see pages 77 and 79). The drawings were
successfully shown at the Leicester Galleries. Nevertheless, Rackham
was somewhat shaken and disappointed by the adverse criticism he
received, and he did not proceed to illustrate *Through The Looking-
Glass*, although Macmillan (Lewis Carroll's original publishers)
offered in 1907 to produce his illustrations of the *Looking-Glass*
before the copyright had expired, in a uniform edition with Heinemann's *Alice* – a remarkable gesture of confidence.
Rackham's model for Alice was Doris (Jane) Dommett, who told
the story of her sittings to the *Evening News* (14th December 1939)
after Rackham's death. 'He chose me from a number of little girls,'

'Fairies never say, "We feel happy": what they say is, "We feel *dancey*" ' *Peter Pan in Kensington Gardens* (by courtesy of Hodder and Stoughton Ltd).

said Miss Dommett, 'and I was so pleased he copied my print frock exactly, because it was one my mother had allowed me to design myself. The woollen stockings I wore were knitted by my old French nannie Prudence. They were thick, to keep out the cold, and how they tickled!' In the mad tea-party picture she sat in Rackham's big wing-back chair, and the table was laid with Mrs Rackham's best china. The Rackhams' kitchen, and their cook, contributed to the kitchen scene. Miss Dommett remembered asking doubtfully: 'Will she throw plates?' 'Oh, no,' said Rackham, 'they've been broken already.' He had actually thrown a few to get the detail right.

The illustrations for *A Midsummer-Night's Dream* (see pages 81, 85, 89), exhibited at the Leicester Galleries and published by Heinemann in 1908, and also in American, French and German editions, were much

The Blackwall tunnel: 'our artist
equipped for the tunnel'.
A self-portrait of 1894.

'A Mad Tea Party.' *Alice's Adventures in Wonderland*, 1907.

77

less controversial in theme than *Alice*, and their success was un-grudged, though Rackham's art was now receiving a measure of that severe scrutiny which comes to every artist who is popular with the general public. Rackham cast his spell over the play; his drawings superseded the work of all his predecessors from Gilbert to Abbey, and for fifty years have enriched the imagination; his conception of Puck and Bottom, Titania and Oberon, Helena and Hermia, his gnarled trees and droves of fairies, have represented the visual reality of the *Dream* for thousands of readers. Here he excelled especially in landscape, and in reconciling dream and reality, giving himself to the luxury of rich detail with a rare generosity. It is scarcely too much to mention him in the same breath as Mendelssohn; but a contemporary and more exact musical comparison might be made, as Eric Blom has suggested, with the delicate fancy of Roger Quilter.

William de Morgan, in a letter to Rackham, described his *Mid-summer-Night's Dream* as 'the most splendid illustrated work of the century, so far'. Rackham's success with books of this kind was now beginning to attract competitors, one of whom was Edmund Dulac whose drawings for *The Tempest* followed Rackham's *Dream* draw-ings at the Leicester Galleries in 1908. Rackham's junior by fifteen years, Dulac had no doubt been influenced by him, but his art was in contrast to Rackham's in several respects. Dulac's inspiration was primarily oriental, better suited to the *Arabian Nights* than to Shake-speare, while Rackham belonged to the Western, even the nordic world; Dulac's emphasis lay in colour harmonies, while Rackham's was in line, to which he skilfully added colour washes of transparent tints – a method well suited to reproduction and virtually a personal invention of his own. The appearance of two such gifted artists in this special field gave English illustrated books a world-wide reputa-tion in the years before the First World War.

As Johnson said of Shakespeare, so we may say of King Edward VII: 'Fairies in his time were much in fashion.' 1909 was the year that

'The Queen turned angrily away from him and said to the Knave
"Turn them over." ' *Alice's Adventures in Wonderland,* 1907.

saw the production of Maeterlinck's *The Blue Bird* with Norman O'Neill's music at the Haymarket Theatre – there were suggestions that Rackham should illustrate *The Blue Bird*, but unfortunately he never did – and in this year Constable issued the final edition of Rackham's *Grimm's Fairy Tales* and Heinemann his illustrated edition of De la Motte Fouqué's *Undine* (see pages 91 and 93). Although the waves and eddies of *Undine* bear the mark of Art Nouveau, the work was still another step forward for Rackham, the unity of conception in the line drawings and the colour plates, the assertion of contrast in the moods of the heroine, rendering it a masterpiece of sympathetic understanding.

Rackham had become a public figure. Writers, well-known and less well-known, continually invited him to illustrate their works; but, as his time was pledged for years ahead, they were usually disappointed. He was now the father of a small daughter, Barbara, born in 1908, and the descendant of schoolmasters spoke out to insist that children deserved only the best in art. The *Daily Mirror* (24th November 1908) printed photographs of ugly dolls that Rackham had condemned and of pretty dolls that he had approved, and showed a photograph of him and Barbara with a toy rabbit that he thought 'very good'. Later he gave an American encyclopaedia, *The Junior Book of Authors* (1934), his credo in the matter of children's art:

'I can only say that I firmly believe in the greatest stimulating and educative power of imaginative, fantastic, and playful pictures and writings for children in their most impressionable years – a view that most unfortunately, I consider, has its opponents in these matter of fact days. Children will make no mistakes in the way of confusing the imaginative and symbolic with the actual. Nor are they at all blind to decorative or arbitrarily designed treatment in art, any more than

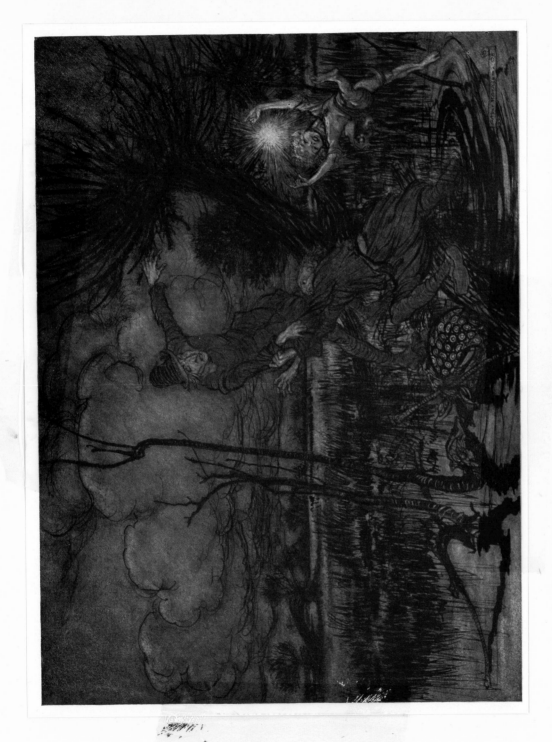

'Mislead night-wanderers, laughing at their harm?' *A Midsummer-Night's Dream*, 1908.

they are to poetic or rhythmic form in literature. And it must be insisted on that nothing less than the best that can be had, cost what it may (and it can hardly be cheap) is good enough for those early impressionable years when standards are formed for life. Any accepting, or even choosing, art or literature of a lower standard, as good enough for children, is a disastrous and costly mistake.'

Many of Rackham's correspondents were children, whose letters he always answered with the utmost courtesy and patience. Three who wrote to him from Kensington in the autumn of 1909 were Betty, Joan and Gilbert Simon, the children of John Simon, K.C., as he then was (Viscount Simon as he eventually became). The young Simons had been reading *The Wind in the Willows*, which had

A letter from Rackham,
26 October 1909.

16, CHALCOT GARDENS,
SOUTH HAMPSTEAD. N.W.

26 Oct 09

My dear Betty, Joan & Gilbert
    Very many thanks for your kind letter. I was most pleased that you thought of me when you were reading the 'Wind in the Willows'
    Curiously enough I very nearly did illustrate it. The publishers asked me to, but at the time it would have had to be done, I was too busy illustrating the Midsummer Nights Dream.
    But its a splendid book, isn't it! The little field mice singing carols are among the jolliest things in it. I specially like

recently been published, with only a frontispiece by Graham Robertson as illustration, and they were anxious that Arthur Rackham should illustrate it – particularly the incident of the field-mice singing carols. Rackham's reply, which is reproduced below, ends with an amusing self-portrait and reveals him as an early admirer of *The Wind in the Willows*. He had been the author's choice as the illustrator, but had had to refuse, reluctantly, owing to pressure of other work. Hence the fact that the illustrations most usually associated with Kenneth Grahame's masterpiece are E. H. Shepard's. It was not until nearly thirty years later that Rackham got another chance to illustrate *The Wind in the Willows*, when an American publisher commissioned a delightful set of drawings from him, which have a special charm born of long affection. They are the last drawings he ever made.

when they toasted their chilblains till they tingled — (but perhaps you've never had chilblains? Well, don't!)

And Toad is grand, isn't he!

I suppose you know that the frontispiece is by the same clever man who wrote the play 'Pinkie & the Fairies' which perhaps you saw or will see.

I am rather afraid that a great deal of the work I am doing now is really for grown-ups. But I have just finished illustrating Grimm's Fairy Tales which I began many years ago, really before you were born, & have gone on adding to the number of pictures until now that

it is just going to be published.

It's a little earlier than customary but I think I had better seize this opportunity of wishing you a Merry Christmas all!

And so good bye from

Yours ever

Arthur Rackham

A friend who had been another Edwardian child, Margaret Andrewes, tells an anecdote which shows Rackham's willingness to entertain the young:

'He came to the house when I was a small girl and my parents were out. As usual, he was at once given a sketchbook and paints, and, as usual, asked what he was to draw. Just then my mother came back from a funeral, heard the question and said, "Anything but a funeral". So Arthur Rackham started with an ant in the bottom left-hand corner of the page, went on to a large area of cobblestones, put in some feet (because the ant must have something to look at), and then the bodies above the feet – two lugubrious figures in black. Then he apologised that it *was* turning into a funeral and, last of all, put in the little parson in the distance, closing the gates of the cemetery. The result is a most treasured possession. . . .'

Barbara was to find him a good father in all sorts of ways, a really interesting and knowledgeable guide to books, museums, corners of London, and so on – and of course always ready and eager to draw anything and everything on demand. When as a child she ran into his room in the morning, he would first feel on the bedside table for his spectacles, then under the pillow for his gold hunter watch; flicking it open, he would look at the time – 'Too early – go back to bed for – er – forty minutes!' or 'All right – in you come, Rabbits!' He made a complete stage set and characters for Cinderella for her German toy theatre. He was fond of all inventive games, and never minded being invaded in his studio, in fact people and conversation around him never disturbed him while he was working. Barbara would often watch him at work, sitting at his drawing desk, with a paint brush in his mouth while he used a pen, or vice versa, making the weird grimaces of his characters as he drew them – a fascinating performance for a child.

'Sleep thou, and I will wind thee in my arms.' *A Midsummer-Night's Dream*, 1908.

85

As a return for all this entertainment, Barbara, in course of time, had to pose for her father. 'Go on – get over there – bend over and pick up an apple,' he would say; 'hold your skirt out with the other hand – put your leg further in front, no, the other one – and now twist round towards me and shake your hair over your shoulder – that's it – now stay still.' And then, after what seemed an eternity – 'All right, you can drop the pose – but now get up on that chair and see if you can be another child throwing the apples down from the tree.'

'Oscar', and Miss Marie Tempest. Two drawings from *W.B.*, 11 January 1895.

CHAPTER FIVE

The Impact of 1914

ON 31st January 1910, the Authors' Club paid Rackham the compliment of entertaining him at dinner in Whitehall Court. The occasion served to emphasize his standing as the leading illustrator of the day, and was reported to the extent of a column and a half in the *Morning Post*. A large gathering applauded his 'random thoughts of an illustrator'. The artist knew, said Rackham, that 'for his illustrations to be worth anything he must be regarded as a partner, not as a servant'.

'. . . An illustration may legitimately give the artist's view of the author's ideas; or it may give his view, his independent view, of the author's subject. But it must be the artist's view; any attempt to coerce him into a mere tool in the author's hands can only result in the most dismal failure. Illustration is as capable of varied appeal as is literature itself; and the only real essential is an association that shall not be at variance or unsympathetic. The illustrator is sometimes expected to say what the author ought to have said or failed to say clearly, to fill up a shortcoming, and not infrequently he has done so. Sometimes he is wanted to add some fresh aspect of interest to a subject which the author has already treated interestingly from his point of view, a partnership that has often been productive of good. But the most fascinating form of illustration consists of the expression by the artist of an individual sense of delight or emotion aroused by the accompanying passage of literature.'

Rackham's surviving correspondence shows that he was now in touch with almost as many authors as artists. There are letters in these and later years from Laurence Housman, Edmund Gosse, Alfred Noyes, Arthur Symons, Rudyard Kipling (whose *Puck of Pook's Hill* he illustrated for an American edition), Maurice Hewlett, James Stephens, Eden Phillpotts. Much of his correspondence related to commissions that eventually matured; more, perhaps, to abortive projects that came to nothing. And occasionally there are isolated notes, not easily explained, that provokingly suggest the width of his acquaintanceship, as with the following postcard from Bernard Shaw:

'Ayot St. Lawrence, Welwyn, Herts.   15th March, 1911.

'I am afraid I can't say Yes or No straight off – that is, if you can leave the question of my coming open. I have had an accident which has disabled my motor car. If it can be repaired in time to take me out of town on Sunday morning I can stay over Saturday night. If not, I must go away by train on Saturday afternoon. If I can come, may I bring my wife?

'I am greatly hurt at your calling me a slight acquaintance. I regard you as quite an old pal.

'I adore Sumurun.

'Many thanks for the invitation.

G. B. S.'

In the years before the 1914 war the Rackhams lived a full social life, entertaining their literary and artistic friends at dinner-parties and

'To hear the sea-maid's music.' *A Midsummer-Night's Dream*, 1908.

'At Homes'. 'Sumurun', adored by Shaw, was apparently a dancer who performed at Mrs Rackham's 'At Homes'. Holidays were usually spent on the Continent, especially in Germany, where they visited Bayreuth for the Wagner festival, and in Switzerland. In 1909 they went to Spain; and in that year Rackham enlarged his circle by becoming a member of the Art-Workers' Guild. Thereafter he was a regular attender at the Guild's meetings.

His work was exhibited almost annually at this time in one or other of the cities of Europe. He won a gold medal in Milan as early as 1906. In 1912 he won a medal at Barcelona and held a special exhibition in Paris of his Wagner drawings at the invitation of the Société Nationale des Beaux Arts, which made him an Associate and awarded him another gold medal. Works by Rackham were acquired for the galleries at Vienna and Barcelona, and for the Luxembourg, Paris.

He was now receiving letters from admirers all over the world. Those that came from children always gave him pleasure; he replied to them straightforwardly and seriously, without any 'talking down' to his youthful correspondents. (This accorded to his usual practice in conversation with children.) In 1910, for example, a little girl entirely unknown to him, Rachel Fry, aged twelve, who loved his books, thought that it would be wonderful if Arthur Rackham could come to stay with her at her home near Ipswich. She received the following reply:

'16 Chalcot Gardens, South Hampstead, N.W.   21 Sep. 1910.

'My dear Miss Fry,
    'I should have answered your kind letter before, but that I have been away from home for a few weeks – and not so very far from where you live, as I have been at Walberswick on the Suffolk coast.
    'It is very kind of you to want me to come & stay with you, but I

'The Knight took the beautiful girl in his arms and bore her over the narrow space where the stream had divided her little island from the shore.' *Undine*, a drawing of 1909.

am afraid I cannot manage to do that though I know I should enjoy it. But I am kept so busy at home over my books & pictures that I have not time to accept half the kind invitations I receive.

'I am very glad you like my illustrations. I am rather afraid that the books of mine that are coming out this year & next, which illustrate Wagner's great Music-stories, the "Ring of the Nibelungs", are not very well suited for those lucky people who haven't yet finished the delightful adventure of growing up, but soon, perhaps, you will know & be fond of Wagner's music and writings, & then you may like these drawings of mine as well as the others.

'Believe me,
Sincerely yours
Arthur Rackham'

The Wagner illustrations that Rackham had been working on and which appeared in two parts in 1910 and 1911 as *The Rhinegold and The Valkyrie* and *Siegfried and The Twilight of the Gods* (see page 95), represented an important achievement for him. It cannot be denied that Rackham was to some extent the victim of his own success in the Christmas book trade, and of his mastery of the technical process of colour reproduction. His genius for fanciful improvisation appeared so inexhaustible – for he was remarkably consistent in his patient application to his craft – that it was all too easy to undervalue him as an artist of the creative imagination. Yet there are many drawings throughout his best books, such as *Rip, Peter Pan*, or the *Dream*, which reveal to the discerning what an original artist he was (and the tail-pieces and other decorations in the text must not be overlooked in this search). The drawings for Wagner gave him above all a theme – the Norse Myths – which appealed to his nordic sympathies, and with it a series of noble motives. Although the heroic did not really suit his talent, his gods and Rhine-maidens were realized on a high plane of imagination, probably because Wagner had deeply

' "Little niece," said Kühleborn, "forget not that I am here with thee as a guide." '
Undine, a drawing of 1909.

93

stirred him personally. To take one example that could easily be overlooked, his title-page of the Rhine-maidens and Nibelungs supporting the Ring, reproduced on the title-page of this book, is a brilliantly successful and truly inventive design. When some of these drawings were exhibited at the Leicester Galleries in a room adjacent to drawings by another distinguished illustrator, Hugh Thomson, the latter appeared remarkably trivial.

Rackham's determination to maintain and to raise the standard of his work was incessant. As he had written a few years earlier (10th December 1906) to M. H. Spielmann, who had drawn his attention to a favourable criticism: 'I've just seen the Graphic & I blush. Well, I can only do my best to live up to it. But the farther I go (& I do hope I am gaining ground) the harder it becomes & the more impossible the "arrival".'

The Rackham books published in 1912 and 1913 made a complete contrast to Wagner. In *Aesop's Fables* (1912) and *Mother Goose* (1913) Rackham's primary intention was to amuse, but his illustrations for the fables of 'The Moon and her Mother' and 'The Gnat and the Lion' suggest the imaginative refinement that he brought to the task. Rackham was often his own model; there are several self-caricatures to be detected in *Aesop's Fables*. He is the man who catches the flea, the pompous gentleman who scolds the drowning boy, the credulous slave-owner who scrubs the black boy (see page 101).

The *Mother Goose* drawings, illustrating a collection of the old nursery rhymes, appeared in the American *St Nicholas Magazine*, 1912–13. Here Rackham laid himself out to please the children, and was completely successful. The initial letters at the beginning of each chapter of this biography are taken from *Mother Goose,* Rackham himself figuring in the initial I at the opening of the first chapter. The House that Jack Built, shown on the next page of text, was a drawing of his own home in Chalcot Gardens.

Aesop's Fables and *Mother Goose* are small books that have had a

'Nothung! Nothung! Conquering sword!' Frontispiece from *Siegfried and The Twilight of the Gods,* 1911 (by courtesy of the Hon. Lady Nicolson, C.H.).

large sale, and at the time of writing are still in print. Unfortunately many of Rackham's larger volumes published during these years now have to be sought in the second-hand book-sellers' shops (where they are expensive to buy), among them the delightful *Arthur Rackham's Book of Pictures* (1913), which is of particular biographical interest. For the most part this was a collection of unpublished work, though a number of the forty-four coloured illustrations had been previously published in magazines or periodicals, usually as first sketches in black and white. At least one of the water-colours, 'Elfin Revellers', which dates from 1900 and suggests the influence of Alma-Tadema, might have been better omitted; but Rackham did well to include several sketches, virtually unaltered, which had originated in the two-hour sessions on Friday evenings at the Langham Sketching Club. A single coloured drawing for one of his books would normally take him several days; but these Langham sketches show how quickly and effectively he could work against the clock when it was necessary for him to do so.

Arthur Rackham's Book of Pictures brings together a number of drawings unrelated in theme. Most of them, it is true, are drawings of

'This is the house that Jack built.' A drawing of 16 Chalcot Gardens, reproduced in *Mother Goose*, 1913.

'There was an old woman
Lived under a hill.'
Mother Goose, 1913: a drawing of 1912.

the supernatural, of goblins, elves and fairies, and many are based on actual fairy tales; but there are also delightful straightforward drawings of children at the seaside or in the Broad Walk, Kensington Gardens; there is the well-known 'Cupid's Alley' (see page 59), which illustrates verses by Austin Dobson, and there are subject pictures and landscapes of wide variety. It was important that such a book should be drawn together by an introductory essay, and natural for Rackham to invite Barrie to write it. The answer he received was cordial but disappointing:

'3, Adelphi Terrace House, Strand, W.C.   24 June 1913.

'Dear Rackham,
    'I wish I could, but I have promised to write two introductions this autumn, and had better not undertake more. Added to which I would be very bad at it as I have no skill in criticism. I am very glad to hear of the book and look forward to it. You have no greater admirer than myself, and few there are more warmly indebted to you.
                                        'Yours very sincerely
                                        J. M. Barrie'

Rackham was fortunate in obtaining Sir Arthur Quiller-Couch as a substitute for Barrie. 'Q' not only admired Rackham's work; he also thoroughly understood a child's instinctive longing for the imaginative and fanciful. 'To this instant, constant, intellectual need of childhood no one in our day,' he wrote, 'has ministered so bountifully or so whole-heartedly as Mr Rackham.' And Quiller-Couch was happy, too, in associating the random, impressionistic nature of much of the *Book of Pictures* with 'the wayward visions that tease every true artist's mind, while he bends over the day's work'.

    'As one who has been doing the day's work in another form of art, and for more years than he cares to count, I wish it were possible for

'The man in the wilderness asked me
How many strawberries grew in the sea.'
                                    Mother Goose.

99

someone to make for me such a collection of fugitive impressions, hints of beauty, threads caught and followed (often tenaciously) only to be lost in the end; scraps of song; stories that after one bright apparition faded away into limbo. They would make one's best biography. . . . Mr Rackham has been more fortunate, and I congratulate him. But let the purchaser who, turning these pages, may happen to wish that they told a connected story, reflect that he may have hold of something better worth his money; the elusive dreams of an artist such as the goblin in Hans Andersen saw and adored for the moment as he peered down the chimney into the student's garret over the huckster's shop; the dreams of an artist who has taught English children in our time to see that

> '*All things by immortal power,*
> *Near or far,*
> *Hiddenly*
> *To each other linkèd are,*
> *That thou canst not stir a flower*
> *Without troubling of a star.*'

The chance survival of a set of block-maker's proofs of the year 1913 affords an opportunity of considering in detail Rackham's meticulous labours for *Mother Goose* and the *Book of Pictures*. So particular was he about the colour reproduction of his work that he would often send the proofs back and forth many times. He studied the technique with deep seriousness, and would even alter his own use of colour in an attempt to limit himself to those colours which reproduced most faithfully.

The first proof for his illustration in *Mother Goose* (see page 99) of

> '*The man in the wilderness asked me*
> *How many strawberries grew in the sea. . . .*'

'Adrift.' *Arthur Rackham's Book of Pictures*, 1913: a drawing of 1909 illustrating Hans Andersen's *The Snow Queen* (by courtesy of W. Mostyn-Owen, Esq.).

The outbreak of war in 1914 found Rackham, approaching his forty-seventh birthday, inundated with work and commissions. The war years did not prove easy for him. The quality of book-production inevitably declined. In 1915 his earnings dropped considerably, though they gradually increased again. He contributed generously to many publications of a patriotic nature – to *King Albert's Book* (1914); to *Princess Mary's Gift Book* (1914); to *The Queen's Gift Book* (1915), published in aid of Queen Mary's Convalescent Auxiliary Hospitals – and he also illustrated *The Allies' Fairy Book,* which appeared in 1916 with an introduction by Edmund Gosse. There was a little dinner at the Windham Club in April of that year, at which Gosse entertained Asquith, Lord Newton, Haddon Chambers (the playwright), Arthur Rackham, and others. And when *The Allies' Fairy Book* was published, Gosse wrote to Rackham (6th November 1916): 'Will you think me impertinent if I tell you how beautiful I think your illustrations. . . . Their variety, and ingenuity, and the delicacy of your fancy, and the romantic ardour of your mind, were never more victoriously manifested. I am proud to be associated – though to so humble a degree – in a work so charming.'

It was typical of Rackham that he should not be content with serving his country as an artist. Like Keene in an earlier emergency, he had to serve also as a man. A self-caricature (reproduced here) on the fly-leaf of a copy of *The Queen's Gift Book,* which he gave to his sister-in-law Ruth Rackham, shows him standing at ease with oriental inscrutability in the grey cotton uniform of the Hampstead Volunteers. Mr Gilbert Foyle writes of those days:

'I was then (1915) Sergeant Major of the Company, and it was great fun to see him endeavouring to do the "Army Drill". He found difficulty in "forming fours", and at rifle drill was a scream. But he was a good recruit, and did his best to please and to learn. He enjoyed going with the Company on Sundays to dig trenches in Essex, near Chelmsford."

The war years held other worries for Rackham. His wife now became seriously ill, from a heart attack after pneumonia. She never recovered her full health but suffered from cardiac and nervous weakness for the rest of her life. Her painting had to be almost entirely abandoned.

A large part of the war was spent by Mrs Rackham and her daughter in furnished houses at Rustington, near Littlehampton, while her husband remained at 16, Chalcot Gardens, paying them visits when he could. In this way Edyth Rackham avoided the strain of the 1914–18 air raids, which, though overshadowed by the bombing of

An informal self-portrait at the time of Rackham's war service in January 1916.

the Second World War, were sufficiently disturbing in their time. Rackham's undated letters to her describe the 'bomb-craters on Parliament Hill', the clatter of the anti-aircraft guns and the dangers of falling shrapnel: 'I went to Wandsworth [*where his mother and two sisters lived*] yesterday. And right through town from here the road is full of groups of kneeling children with all manner of tools gouging & digging out the shrapnel from the wood pavement. Our guns keep going like hell.' Inspecting the row of craters at the foot of Parliament Hill, near Gospel Oak, he talked to a man who had been in the Duke of St Albans' public house when the bombs fell: 'He says that it was all over before you knew. Bang! the glass in! Silence. The broken gas main flared up outside – but nothing much, he says. No time to be frightened. He didn't appear to have minded in the least. A man of 55 or so.' (Thus Cockney sang-froid, anticipating the 'blitz' of 1940.) A letter to his daughter of 1917 shows Rackham as a grass widower indeed, trying to cut the neglected lawn and prune the overgrown trees in his garden.

Rackham worked steadily through all these disturbances, and, apart from numerous minor publications of ephemeral interest, produced several books of lasting value during the war years. He is not usually remembered as an illustrator of Dickens, but *A Christmas Carol* (1915) was decidedly successful, for he contrived to adapt the tradition of 'Phiz' and Cruikshank to his own characteristic style in the pictures of Victorian London (see page 107) and at the same time found scope for his fantasy in the ghost scenes. We also find him here developing his special talent for silhouette, rare among illustrators. That he only once attempted Dickens again – with *The Chimes* for the Limited Editions Club in 1931 – may be a matter for regret, for he was well qualified by sympathy to interpret Dickens in certain of his moods.

With *Little Brother and Little Sister* (1917), Rackham added forty more stories by the Brothers Grimm to the sixty which he had already

'"What do you call this?" said Joe. "Bed-curtains!"' *A Christmas Carol*, 1915.

illustrated, his inspiration showing no decline. His drawings for Swinburne's poems of childhood, *The Springtide of Life* (1918), again attracted the admiration of Edmund Gosse, who expressed his appreciation in a preface and told Rackham personally (18th October 1918): 'This volume will not merely be the best book of the present art-season, but a joy to all sensitive people for years and years to come.' It may nevertheless be doubted whether Rackham was at his best with baby worship on such an intensive scale. The immediate aftermath of the war brought *Some British Ballads* (1919), and the two volumes of *Cinderella* (1919) and *The Sleeping Beauty* (1920), retold by C. S. Evans, in which his gift for silhouette was given full play (see pages 110 and 111).

It was during these years that Rackham was most active in the Art-Workers' Guild. He served on its committee in 1917–18, and in 1919 followed such distinguished predecessors as Walter Crane, William Morris, Sir George Clausen and W. R. Lethaby into the Master's chair. Among the lectures at which he presided in his year of office were several whose subjects reflected his interests – notably those on 'Modern methods of Process Reproduction', 'Colour Lithography' and 'Fairy-tale Illustrations'. The Guild also held an exhibition of Art for Children during this year.

A writer in the *Sunday Times* after Rackham's death remembered that in the discussions which followed the fortnightly papers 'he spoke with quiet decision and an elusive sense of humour that showed itself in a twinkling eye and a dry smile'. He served the Guild with scrupulous devotion. A self-portrait in oils, dated 1924, hangs in the hall of the Guild to remind a later generation of what manner of man he was. It shows him wearing a bow-tie and a grey waistcoat; he holds a pencil in one hand, a sketch-book in the other. There is nothing smug about this face, of which the lines are sensitive and thoughtful to the point of severity (in Rackham's case an introspective exaggeration). The background shows the River Thames, Waterloo Bridge

DON
QUIXOTE
AND
THE
INNKEEPER

Mr Irving as Don Quixote. *W.B.*, 13 September 1895.

Above and opposite: silhouette illustration from *The Sleeping Beauty*,

1920. Some of the silhouettes in this book were printed in three colours.

III

and the Shot Tower. Another self-portrait (the frontispiece of this book) painted in 1934, may be thought more successful in suggesting the kindly amusing man behind the mask. This again has a London background – St Paul's Cathedral. Rackham was always proud to call himself a Cockney. Indeed, he took care to make the further distinction that he had been born *south* of the Thames. The self-portrait of 1934, when exhibited at the Royal Society of Portrait Painters, bore the explanatory title 'A Transpontine Cockney'.*

Although in 1919 he was preparing to 'twitch his mantle blue' and make for new pastures beside the River Arun, he kept a studio in London until almost the end of his life.

* Rackham was painted by Meredith Frampton, R.A., in 1920, but this portrait was destroyed with a large part of Mr Frampton's studio in 1940.

CHAPTER SIX

American Friends

RACKHAM'S habitual costume was a navy-blue suit with a stiff white collar and a blue-and-white spotted bow-tie. His tailor made him a new suit now and then of exactly the same cut and colour, and the old one was then relegated to his studio. In the last twenty years of his life he ventured a few concessions to the rôle of the well-to-do country gentleman, and even for a while sported a tweed suit, but those who knew him best felt that this never seemed quite in character.

It was in 1920 – a year of almost fabulous prosperity for Rackham, when his earned income, with the help of the proceeds of American exhibitions, touched seven thousand pounds – that he acquired his first country home, a Georgian flint farmhouse at Houghton, near Arundel. Houghton House, warm, dignified and beautiful, faced the village street immediately opposite the George and Dragon Inn. The garden offered wide views over the Downs and the Arun valley, and gave on to fields sloping to the River Arun, where Rackham used to fish. He was fond of fly-fishing, a sport unknown to that river, and sometimes collected an incredulous crowd to watch him casting over the water. The only fish he could catch there with a fly were small, rather muddy dace. He taught his daughter to clean and cook these in the ashes of a bonfire on the bank.

The purchase of Houghton House meant the sale of 16, Chalcot Gardens, but for his London studio Rackham now acquired 6, Primrose Hill Studios (close to the first home of his married life). At Houghton his studio was a thatched converted barn.

Rackham's country neighbours proved a congenial mixture of farmers, artists and retired colonels. There were tennis parties on slow erratic grass courts; boating parties up the Arun backwaters; fancy-dress dances in gardens decorated with fairy lights and Chinese lanterns. On summer weekends, when Mrs Rackham was well enough, Houghton House was often filled with artist friends from the London days. It was a primitive house by modern standards, with a well in the wash-house, no main water, candles instead of electric light, and rats scurrying up and down the hollow walls at night.

The inconveniences were cheerfully accepted by Rackham, who had no liking for modern inventions. While he admitted to an affection for the bicycle, it was a favourite assertion of his that the fall of man began with the invention of the wheel. He would never have become a motorist if his wife, increasingly a semi-invalid, had not discovered a passion for being driven round the countryside for thirty miles a day at thirty miles an hour in the back seat of an open car. Reluctantly compelled to use 'that infernal machine the telephone', he considered photography, the cinema and the wireless to be degradations of art, and it was as well that he did not have to reckon with television.

Although he appreciated good company and was drawn out by it into joviality, Rackham by nature was a quiet man with simple tastes and an abstemious, almost austere attitude to life. No doubt owing to his straitened circumstances in early years, he was unable easily to spend money on pleasure. For him, however prosperous he became, the only really legitimate excuses for spending were health and education. He firmly believed in the essential rightness of working and saving for the fundamentals of existence.

Trilby on the stage: Mr Tree as Svengali. *W.B.*, 13 September 1895.

At some time he did acquire the habit of a nightly glass of Marsala. This he enjoyed to the last. Any other form of drinking he considered a luxury, though he was not unappreciative of an occasional bottle of wine. He did not smoke. He had no very advanced appreciation of the pleasures of the table. His favourite meal was cold roast beef. An influential art dealer and prospective buyer once found him in his London studio, at three o'clock in the afternoon, eating sardines off a newspaper. When Rackham cheerfully described the encounter to his wife, Mrs Rackham was horrified. Rackham believed, incidentally, in the virtues of newspaper for all sorts of uses – as blotting-paper, as wrapping, for keeping warm in bed, for filing (his correspondence, notes, etc., were neatly collected in folded copies of *The Times,* labelled in chalk on the outside), for drying out damp shoes, as a tablecloth. . . .

Perhaps the indulgence that pleased him most was to travel abroad, very simply, walking or cycling with a man friend, always with a sketch-book in his pocket. He spent several sketching holidays in Italy, and almost (but not quite) became a Roman Catholic after one visit to Assisi.

The simplicity of his life helped Rackham to keep remarkably fit for his age. To the younger members of the Daleham Lawn Tennis Club, St John's Wood – where Rackham used to play in the early nineteen-twenties – he naturally appeared quite an old man. But his energy amazed them. Mr George E. Heath remembers it:

'He would come to the club looking rather wizened and very like one of his own dwarf drawings, and would play tennis – he was an average club player – for about three hours without stopping. After about six sets, he would leave with only the briefest of farewells to any of the other members. He took, as far as I can remember, practically no part in the club's social activities, but was always extremely popular, and greatly admired for his fantastic energy and enthusiasm.'

Olive trees above Assisi (by courtesy of Bernard Rackham, Esq., C.B.).

117

For a number of years after 1920 Rackham's output was maintained, and with it his high earning power, which was now considerably supplemented by an income from investments. In 1920 came his illustrations for *Irish Fairy Tales* by the poet James Stephens, who told Rackham that it was 'a great pleasure' and 'a great privilege' to work with him. Walter Starkie recalls one evening from their friendship:

'Arthur Rackham considered drawing a more important accomplishment for his daughter than writing, for drawing was more natural: it was like dancing to the rhythms that spring up spontaneously in a child's mind. Barbara when a tiny tot danced one evening in the garden for James Stephens who was with us. I fiddled an Irish fairy reel and the little sylph-like figure with her fair hair glistening in the moonbeams flitted here and there under the trees, while the poet intoned softly his poem "The Whisperer":

> *The Moon was round!*
> *And, as I walked along,*
> *There was no sound,*
> *Save when the wind with long*
> *Low hushes whispered to the ground*
> *A snatch of Song.'*

Remembering another occasion when Augustus John was present, Walter Starkie sees John and Rackham, in his mind's eye, 'as Big Claus and Little Claus, and between them I spy the diminutive Pan-like figure of James Stephens seated cross-legged upon a table thrumming a guitar and gazing wistfully at the two painters'.

The appearance of Eden Phillpotts's *A Dish of Apples* brought a characteristically appreciative letter from its author (24th September 1921): 'I am immensely pleased at the charm & originality of your most attractive drawings. The humour of them especially drew me.' Rackham was achieving a new harmony of colour, his drawings for *A Dish of Apples,* to quote an American admirer Martin Birnbaum, being 'light and sparkling with passionate rose, glowing greens and primrose yellow'. Another, more important, publication of Rackham's in 1921 was a long-delayed edition of Milton's *Comus,* the drawings for which, begun before the war, deserve to rank with his best work of that earlier period, though it is an uneven book. Rackham here ran the gamut of his artistic emotions. The 'rout of Monsters' provoked him to several disconcerting drawings in what was for him an unusually disturbing vein, exploited again later in his illustrations for Poe. Beardsley's influence marks several pages of *Comus*; yet these alternate with passages of pure poetry that recall Rackham's own work for *Peter Pan* and the *Dream.*

In 1922 came Hawthorne's *A Wonder Book*; and in 1925 Christopher Morley's *Where the Blue Begins,* which brought the artist the friendship of that most warm-hearted of authors. In 1926 an excitingly original edition of *The Tempest* showed Rackham experimenting in a simplified dramatic technique that was refreshingly and effectively 'modern'.

During the immediate post-war years several old successes, notably *Grimm's Fairy Tales* were revived in separate new editions. Rackham for the first time allowed himself to be tempted into the commercial field by a highly lucrative offer for a series of advertisements from Colgate's in 1922–23–24. An advertisement for Eno's Fruit Salts (1928), a chocolate-box cover for Cadbury's (1933), and covers for book catalogues in the 'thirties represented almost his only other incursions into a sphere that little appealed to his sensibility. He appeared more appropriately, in miniature, in Volume I of *The Book of the Queen's Dolls' House* (1924). And in 1927 Queen Mary bought an illustration of *King Arthur,* 'The Holy Grail', from the R.W.S. Summer Exhibition.

Rackham's work had long had its supporters at the Royal Academy ('I have a great admiration for it personally,' Sir Edward Poynter, P.R.A., had told him in 1916 when urging him to contribute to a special exhibition for the Red Cross). In 1922 he allowed Sir Herbert Hughes-Stanton to put him down for election as an 'Associate Engraver', but, not surprisingly, he lost the ballot to that great engraver H. Macbeth-Raeburn by 26 votes to 11. 'Draughtsmen', as such, were not then admissible as Associates of the Academy. Rackham's candidature may have done something to settle the question of their eligibility for the engraving section, but the rules were not changed until after Rackham's death, and Edward Bawden is still (1960) the only 'draughtsman' so elected.

There is no reason to suppose that Rackham was disturbed by this reverse. Apparently he did retain to the end of his life the lingering remnant of a frustrated youthful ambition to succeed as a painter in oils; but he had realized when he embarked on his career as an illustrator that he would be unlikely to attain the formal honours of the Academy. As compensation he had enjoyed fame, prosperity and the affection of a very wide circle of admirers, young and old.

A more serious cause for disappointment was the increasing difficulty of publishing illustrated books of high quality in England during the 'twenties. The market for fine books was not what it had been in the prosperous decade before 1914. And there was more to it than that. The realities of war had dealt a blow to imaginative craftsmanship in general, and to fairyland in particular. It was a symptom of the changed situation that Rackham's exhibition of recent work at the Leicester Galleries, London, in 1919 was the last that he was to hold there for many years; these exhibitions had been a mutual source of profit to him and to Messrs Ernest Brown and Phillips since 1905, and had played an important part in establishing his reputation.

Fortunately for Rackham, the changed situation in England coincided with a marked display of enthusiasm for his work in the

The incoming tide. Pencil and watercolour, exhibited at the Leicester Galleries in 1916 (by courtesy of Mrs Harris Rackham).

United States. The Rackham books, both in their limited and their trade editions, had long established themselves in the book-collectors' market on both sides of the Atlantic, but it is noticeable that there was now a considerable increase in the number of letters he received from American publishers, collectors, and simple admirers. In 1923, for example, a group of students at the Senior High School, Trenton, New Jersey, chose him, as a 'noted man' whose life had made 'an especial appeal to them', to be a 'sort of "guardian" ' for them; and they begged 'a little letter of kindly interest'. Rackham responded gallantly after a pause for thought: 'If you possibly can, be makers & not dealers. Aim at the highest quality in your work. Go on improving it. Never be satisfied with it. Aim at taking pleasure in work for its own sake, & not for what you can make out of it.' It was exactly what he had done himself.

Diving into a pile of surviving 'fan' letters we find one from Rochester, New York, written in the late nineteen-twenties, which commences 'My dear Sir Arthur', and another containing the apology: 'Everybody here in New York calls you "Sir Arthur", and that explains why I began my letter that way.' (A Melbourne correspondent had already asked: 'How shall I begin? Not Mr Rackham surely! It doesn't sound a bit like the artist spirit who creates those wonderful fairy people. . . .') A letter from Texas came from 'a co-ed with red hair and artistic appreciations'. European correspondents, who had long addressed him as 'Dear Master', were surpassed by the Viennese lady who began 'Most Venerated Master . . . please fulfill my passionate wish to me'. Many of the letters, particularly those from isolated parts of America, are moving evidence of the joy which his books brought, particularly to the young and to invalids who could not travel to art galleries.

Rackham's American fame was greatly stimulated by profitable exhibitions of his work held at Scott and Fowles', New York, in 1919, 1920 and 1922. The *New York World*, discussing his *Comus* exhibition in 1922, wrote of him as 'always going ahead, never back-ward'. Americans have pioneered the bibliographical study of Rackham, a field which his industry and the multiplicity of variant editions combine to make exceedingly complex. A short bibliography of Rackham's work by Frederick Coykendall was privately printed in 1922 at Mount Vernon, New York, designed by Bruce Rogers. It was followed fourteen years later by the bibliography compiled by Sarah Briggs Latimore and Grace Clark Haskell, published in Los Angeles, which remains the fullest bibliographical record available.

During the nineteen-twenties it became increasingly clear that Rackham would sooner or later have to accede to the requests of his American admirers that he should come over to 'pick up his laurels'. He went at last in 1927, not only with the object of meeting some of these friends, and of hanging a large exhibition of more than seventy of his works (including the drawings for *The Tempest*) at Scott and Fowles' gallery, New York, but also with the intention of talking business to publishers and editors. Alyn Williams, President of the Royal Society of Miniature Painters, and his American wife were Rackham's companions on the voyage in the liner *Republic* in early November. 'Mrs Williams, thank heaven, had never heard of me before,' Rackham told his wife. In the ship's gymnasium Rackham and Williams went through a series of exercises designed to make Rackham fatter and Williams thinner. These Rackham illustrated in a long letter home. Protesting at a suggestion that he should diet, Williams told the instructor: 'Look at Rackham, talk to him, he eats more than I do.' ('Probably not true,' added Rackham in parentheses). ' "Oh, he may eat what he likes," says the pro: much to Williams' disgust.'

The voyage was smooth, but Rackham found it rather boring and depressing, although he could report: 'The pianist Percy Grainger is on board & played at the concert. . . . He runs round the deck several times before breakfast every day,' an observation that will cause no surprise to the many friends of Grainger. Rackham did not put on much weight; when he reached New York the scales showed 'two pounds under 10 stone'.

He stayed at the Yale Club, and at a first impression New York appeared to him 'surprising and exciting'. His enthusiasm waned when he found it extremely noisy, and the comfortable Yale Club no exception to the rule: 'Oh that brass band – in our hall now. Every third tune is the Wacht am Rhein . . . I imagine Yale must have bagged the tune for a college song. Bang, bang, bang, blare, squeal.' He found 'everything overdone . . . *much* too much – of everything. To live here *must* vulgarise an artist . . . I could *easily* run off & dump my bags & self on the first ship to Europe. . . . Bang bang bang bash. That man will bust that drum if no one stops him.'

Later letters were more cheerful. Rackham at sixty was obviously unable to come to terms with New York, but he found much to enjoy there. 'Everyone is excessively kind,' he wrote; 'Everyone was brought up on my work – if young enough – or brought up their families on it if *old enough*.' He soon had the run of six New York clubs, and was inundated with invitations. 'The nature of my work seems to have made my name familiar to so many others than artists: the bookish people – librarians, book-lovers & so on. . . . The artists are extraordinarily friendly, too. I cannot think any American artist coming to our country (except a Whistler or Sargent) could find himself so heartily greeted.'

Rackham's meetings with many publishers and magazine editors in their 'gorgeous offices' proved satisfactory and productive, though he was disappointed to find that, as in England, 'all the publishers are shy of costly books'. A book-seller encouraged him to 'get together a complete set of all I have ever done. They have sold one such lot for about £400'. He visited Mrs Joseph Pennell, who 'said she thought I was even better known here than in England'. He was introduced to

Gene Tunney, 'an engaging young giant with a gentle handshake'. He went out of town to spend a Sunday with Christopher Morley, 'genial & pleasant & very unaffected', and his wife and four small children. He played bridge at a party with the actress Cissy Loftus, 'quite white-haired now'.

The delay in delivery of letters from his wife worried him, but on a flying visit to Boston he was able to write: 'I'm in much better spirits now I have had your letters, dear dear old Edyth.' His anxiety about her health, and the effect on it of his own absence, drew from him one reassuring letter that was deeply personal: 'Oh my dear old Edyth, it is so difficult for me to make you feel how close close close, how *one* our lives have been for me. How *outside*, how unrecorded, how without influence my wanderings have been to me. . . . The reality of *my* life has been that with you. . . .'

One of the most interesting results of Rackham's trip was a commission from the New York Public Library to provide for the Spencer Collection there a series of special water-colours illustrating *A Midsummer-Night's Dream*. These were exhibited at the Library in 1929, and bound up in a beautiful manuscript book written by Graily Hewitt. The closing days of his stay were spent on a water-colour portrait – 'a handsome young Jewess' – for which he was paid £250. His sitter proved 'very amiable & patient fortunately & anxious that her mother, for whom it is, should have a Christmas present that she will like'.

On his last day in America, before sailing in the *Olympic* at midnight to get home for Christmas, Rackham visited an exhibition of drawings in the Children's Room of the New York Public Library, met the young artist, and spent the evening with him and Anne Carroll Moore, who later described the occasion in *The Horn Book* (Christmas, 1939). He told them he was 'free to kick up my heels until sailing time', so they drove him in a taxi over the Brooklyn and Manhattan bridges to see the lights of the city, took him to supper at the Brevoort Grill, and escorted him on board the *Olympic* with a present of chocolates for his daughter and a candle of good luck to be lit in his cabin.

To have visited the United States and made the acquaintance of so many hitherto unknown admirers remained a lasting source of pleasure to Rackham. Henceforth he often had the American market in mind, as with *The Lonesomest Doll* by Abbie Farwell Brown (1928), which was published only in America, and Washington Irving's *The Legend of Sleepy Hollow* (1928). Many of the drawings for these two books found their way into the collection of Columbia University, New York. In the England of jazz and Noel Coward the whimsical and fantastic had grown increasingly out of fashion. With *The Vicar of Wakefield* of 1929 and *The Compleat Angler* of 1931 (see pages 127 and 131), the frontispiece for which is to be seen at the Victoria and Albert Museum, Rackham played safe by turning to historical costume and river landscape, in which he had long been supremely accomplished and successful.

Altogether, despite some good years and the high prices paid for Rackham originals in America, the post-war period had been somewhat disappointing to one who had made his name in the Edwardian era. Rackham summed up the situation a trifle despondently in a letter to Howard Angus Kennedy of 28th June 1929:

'. . . I need not say what a difference the war has made. The market is now divided up among stacks of cheaply produced & relatively inexpensive books. The "Trades" have so settled it – not without great consideration. And the difficulty of bringing out a rather better book is so great as to be all but prohibitive. I recently went over to the States to see for myself exactly what the conditions were there. And found them much the same. I might tell you of one experience. One of the great firms of New York agreed, after much deliberation,

'A Favourite Song of Dryden's.' *The Vicar of Wakefield*, 1929 (by courtesy of
George G. Harrap & Co. Ltd).

127

to do a book for me: but on hearing that other illustrations of mine were arranged to appear the same season, they at once withdrew their offer. As a matter of fact the better class books do not sell half the number that they did before the war, & there is not as much profit to be made out of each book as there was, so neither publishers nor illustrators are having much of a time. The only men of my craft who are flourishing, are portrait painters, & advertisement designers – branches that I only occasionally enter. . . .'

CHAPTER SEVEN

The Last Years

BY 1929 it had become necessary for the Rackhams to leave
Houghton House, partly because Mrs Rackham's health
was now too precarious for her to be able to cope with
servant problems in the old-fashioned farmhouse, and
partly because Rackham had reluctantly decided that
he was no longer justified in keeping up two establish-
ments, and believed that he would not need to do so if he lived
nearer London. In fact, however, he did not dispose of 6, Primrose
Hill Studios until 1938, a year before his death.

He now built a house in an attractive situation on the Common at
Limpsfield, Surrey, close to the golf course on which he often played.
Stilegate was comfortable, easy to run; the garden was delightful; but
neither Rackham nor his family were entirely happy there. Rackham
naturally missed the surroundings he had loved at Houghton – the
rambling old house with its barns and outhouses, the winding Arun,
the wooded hills, the Amberley quarry, the beech tree with its
knobbly, twisted roots, the magnificent elm, the Elizabethan cottages facing his garden wall – all preserved, here and there, for those
who can recognize them, in his drawings of the nineteen-twenties.

Limpsfield had a suburban conventionality that Rackham grew to
dislike. His new neighbours, friendly enough, were mostly wealthy

business men lacking interest in the arts, with certain notable excep-
tions including Edward and Marjorie Pease, the well-known foun-
der-Fabians and socialists, and his old friends the Keen family. Mrs
Rackham became increasingly an invalid, and hardly went out at all,
except for her motor drives. Few visitors came to the house. More
than ever, Rackham found that he needed his London studio as a
pied-à-terre to bring him into touch with his friends at the Arts Club,
at the R.W.S. or the Art-Workers' Guild.

It would be misleading to show him in his last decade as an un-
happy man, or his wife as totally subdued by ill-health. But it is
undeniable that Mrs Rackham's health, her progress and treatment,
and the various 'cures', orthodox and otherwise, that she tried enthusiastically one after another, absorbed the thoughts of the Stilegate
household. Other interests tended to revolve around this problem.

Rackham worked on as determinedly and enthusiastically as ever.
Harraps were now his principal publishers, and for them he illustrated
Goldsmith and Izaak Walton, Ruskin (*The King of the Golden
River*), Hans Andersen, Christina Rossetti (*Goblin Market*), Brown-
ing (*The Pied Piper of Hamelin*), Edgar Allan Poe, and Ibsen (*Peer
Gynt*). For Harraps, again, he prepared *The Arthur Rackham Fairy
Book*.

His nephew Walter Starkie spent many months in the years
1932–6 wandering through Castile, Andalusia and La Mancha, jour-
neys bearing excellent fruit in his three gypsy books, *Raggle-Taggle*,
Spanish Raggle-Taggle, and *Don Gypsy*, for which Rackham drew
the frontispieces. The gypsies fascinated Rackham; but when Starkie
proposed to his uncle that he should illustrate *Don Quixote*, Rackham was not attracted, saying that the Don appeared so often that
variety was impossible. Starkie suggests that 'Rackham's genius was
so essentially Gothic that it needed the fantastic trees of the forest
and felt ill at ease in the bare steppes of La Mancha'.

The undertaking that meant most to him in the early 'thirties was

'The quietest and fittest place for contemplation.' Frontispiece study of Izaak Walton from *The Compleat Angler*, 1931: George G. Harrap & Co. Ltd.

his edition of Hans Andersen's *Fairy Tales*, a project that had been in his mind for many years (page 135). With Barbara he paid a preparatory visit to Denmark in the autumn of 1931, and while in Copenhagen met an old lady who as a child had hidden under a table in order to hear Andersen himself reading some newly written stories to a gathering of adults. Rackham sketched busily both in town and country, visiting farms and local museums. 'It is rather fatiguing,' he wrote to his wife. 'I have to talk so much & behave myself so well all the while, taking notes & notes for dear life. But everyone is most delightfully friendly & anxious to help. Of course Andersen is their great god. And all, and at the bookshop, are greatly interested in what I have to do.'

At one farm he went into the pigsty. 'But an indoor pigsty. No good for Andersen's Swineherd. And that's a mercy. For the stench was so appalling that I thought I should be sick.'

A deputation of Danes took Rackham and his daughter to visit Hans Andersen's grave. As none of the Danes could speak English, and the Rackhams could not speak Danish, the conversation was entirely in mime. At the graveside one of the deputation startled Rackham by producing a large wreath, which he handed to him with a deferential but purposeful gesture towards the grave. While the Danes stood with bared and bowed heads, Rackham rather sheepishly laid the wreath on the grave. As he did so, he muttered to his daughter, 'This is the sort of thing an Englishman does very badly, I'm afraid!' 'Amen, Amen!' responded the Danes, and replaced their hats.

In a note to his Hans Andersen volume (1932), Rackham emphasized that he had made no attempt in his illustrations 'to look through Danish eyes', but he explained:

'I think that my visit to Denmark, which, with all its modern progress, happily preserves in town and country a genial atmosphere of old dignity in comely everyday use, did give me just that nearer view of the author's country that I needed – a view that helped me to realise again the sensation I felt as a child when I first read Andersen. This sensation experienced in childhood in foreign fairy tales is a foretaste of that encountering of familiar things in unfamiliar guise which later is one of the joys of foreign travel.'

The *Observer* invited Hugh Walpole to choose the best picture-book of 1932. 'I give the prize without hesitation to Rackham's *Hans*

From the invitation card to the 'Daddy and Mummy party'. *W.B.*, 10 January 1896.

Andersen,' Walpole replied. 'He has risen nobly to his subject. He has acquired a new tenderness and grace. His fantasy is stronger than ever.' Twenty-five years after its publication, the *Hans Andersen* had become one of the most difficult of Rackham's books to buy second-hand.

With the *Hans Andersen* may be mentioned *The Arthur Rackham Fairy Book*, undertaken in the same propitious mood and published in the following year. The illustrations were all new, though it was not the first time, as Rackham admitted in his preface, that he had illustrated several of these old favourites of the nursery, 'in the thirty years and more that my work has led me through enchanted lands'.

When we compare these two books with Rackham's achievement in his Edwardian prime, the most remarkable thing to note is that he was maintaining such a consistent standard of excellence at the age of sixty-five. His methods had nevertheless undergone a subtle and almost imperceptible change. There was a slight tendency away from over-all pre-Raphaelite fidelity to detail, and towards a measure of impressionism, at least in the backgrounds. A. S. Hartrick has described* a typical example of Rackham's method in Edwardian days: how he would run a fairly strong tint of raw umber over his pen drawing – except for a few whites when he needed some accents of pure colour in the end. 'This warm tone he lifted with a wet brush as he went along, working in local colour as wanted, while carefully watching the main gradations – warm to cold, and vice versa.' It had been a method helpful to reproduction, giving a pleasing general tone 'like old vellum', and with variations it had served Rackham well. In later years, however, his approach was more flexible and adaptable; a little influence may perhaps be allowed to weakened eyesight; we notice him using cleaner, brighter colours (and his elves and goblins have sharper noses!). Conscious of working for a new generation, Rackham intended to please them as he had pleased their

* In *The Old Water-Colour Society's Club Eighteenth Annual Volume*, 1940.

'When Night was come and the Shop Shut Up.' *Hans Andersen's Fairy Tales*, 1932
(George G. Harrap & Co. Ltd), illustrating *The Goblin and the Provision-dealer*.

135

fathers. Although he would probably have wished posterity to judge him by books such as *Rip Van Winkle* and *Peter Pan*, he was too consistent a craftsman for anyone to be able to speak of a 'falling-off' in the high standard he had set himself.

A letter written to his wife from the Arts Club in 1932 (13th October) gives an impression of Rackham's daily activity while in London. He was then pre-occupied with the business of the Royal Water-Colour Society; he served on its council many times and for three years was a Vice-President; his work had always been an attraction at the Society's exhibitions, and the Society welcomed his advice no less on business affairs than on artistic matters. 'I find I have to be at the R.W.S. on Saturday,' he writes, 'so I shall not be able to come home until Sat. evening. . . . Hanging at the R.W.S. was tiring but I always like doing it and my lecture came off very well.' The next day 'a man from Cadbury's' was coming to see him (about his one-and-only chocolate box), and in the evening there was 'the Harrap dinner'. He supposed that he would 'have to begin settling on next year's book at once', though the trade 'atmosphere' in general seemed 'slower than ever'. He wondered what could be inside the two big parcels which had arrived at Limpsfield for him from Harraps ('sheets to sign, I expect'); he had a word of inquiry for the Limpsfield robins – birds were an increasing interest; and as usual his last thought was for his wife's health: 'Good night, dear old Edy. I hope they do your pillows correctly & that you are sleeping.'

Rackham's portrait of his daughter Barbara – 'a charming head, in tone, with landscape background,' said the critic of *The Times* – hung in the Royal Society of Portrait Painters' exhibition in November 1932. When Barbara brought a friend of hers, the writer R. H. Ward, to Stilegate, Limpsfield, in the summer of the following year, he saw the portrait on the wall of Rackham's studio – 'a building in the garden' (so Mr Ward remembers it), 'separate from the house, separate (one felt) from ordinary affairs, very separate from the politely rural suburb in which it was in any case surprising to find him living, and as retired as a wild creature's den.' Mr Ward thought the portrait 'a recognizable likeness of Barbara Rackham as she was at that time; but the interesting thing was that it made her look much more like her father than she appeared (to me at least) to do in reality; and one had the impression that he had painted himself into it, or in other words that his vision, so highly individual, was as highly subjective'.

This tallied with Mr Ward's general impression of Rackham on that visit to Limpsfield:

'I have the recollection of a smallish, ageing, almost wizened person, with a bald domed forehead and a very wide and elfish grin: a gnome, perhaps, though an entirely benevolent one. But there was more to the impression than that: there was something earthy and even elemental about him. . . . Nor would it be wholly absurd to say that he resembled one of his own grotesquely poetical trees with (as like as not) faces, for which his own face might have served as the

Title-page drawing for *The Children and the Pictures*, 1907.

model. As I've suggested, it was impossible not to be confused as to which was which, the artist himself or the creatures, human, half-human or non-human, of which he had drawn so many. It wasn't in the least that he made one diffident in his presence; one simply couldn't get over seeing so many of his drawings walking about in the shape of one man. It was even surprising that he spoke ordinary English, and not some strange language of fairy-tale or the woods. . . . One of the strongest impressions he gave me was of a person very much "by himself" in every sense. . . .'

A casual visitor's impressions of a stranger will usually bring qualifications or contradictions from those who have known him more intimately – we have seen, for example, that Rackham's isolation, a synonym perhaps for his artistic integrity, was consistent with a strong loyalty and devotion to his family and friends. Yet Mr Ward is not the only chance observer of Arthur Rackham who has retained a similar impression of him. The artist had indeed lived for many years in a world of fantasy that was consistently and recognizably his own. And the relation between the man and his drawings was made particularly close in Rackham's case by his practice of using himself as his own model. Rackham well knew that he was part and parcel of his own creation; and it amused him. Active and supple, he was adept at posing and 'making faces'. His features (or the suggestion of them) are reflected back to us, usually as by a distorting mirror, from the features of innumerable grotesques and from his own personified trees; sometimes they are reflected, as from a clearer mirror, in recognizable self-portraits. Despite his highly developed visual memory for nature and landscape, throughout his life he depended considerably on living models; in addition he kept a large collection of costumes and properties. If a drawing required an attractive woman, no one could satisfy the reader's imagination more delicately or sympathetically than Rackham. Yet his models were often employed merely as human lay figures. One of these models, Marita Ross, has testified (*Everybody's Weekly*, 27th September 1947) that 'a young girl might equally well serve him as the Vicar of Wakefield or an evil old witch. I remember one who even acted as a dismembered corpse . . .'.

Rackham's external life was as reliable and conforming as might be expected of anyone who keeps his accounts, as he did, with Victorian precision. Within the studio, his intense artistic imagination, his love of beauty and of his craft, his power of assimilating himself to nature in all its forms – especially the smaller creation – made him inevitably a man apart. But the Rackham world was one to be created on his own terms of diligent and thoughtful application. Designing for the films or for the theatre might have brought large returns; but the backstage atmosphere of hustle and improvisation was not for him. It was left to Max Reinhardt and Walt Disney to realize on the stage and screen the fantasy that Rackham had so long anticipated, and his one experience of the professional theatre – his costumes and scenery for *Hansel and Gretel* at the Cambridge Theatre, 1933–4 – did not fully satisfy him.

Basil Dean's production of *Hansel and Gretel* which opened on Boxing Day, 1933, with Ernest Irving's arrangement of Humperdinck's score played by members of the London Philharmonic Orchestra, nevertheless had considerable merits. Rackham plunged into his task with boyish enthusiasm; and Alick Johnstone, the scene painter, did full justice to his designs. *Punch* (3rd January 1934) felt that the choice of Rackham as the decorator had been 'a peculiarly happy if, when you come to think of it, obvious inspiration', and described Rackham's forest as 'a scene of authentic theatrical enchantment'. H. E. Wortham in the *Daily Telegraph* (27th December 1933) declared his drop curtain 'a masterpiece with its two impish children so deliciously unselfconscious of being the centre of an elaborate design' (see page 141). If Rackham himself showed less confidence that he had entirely 'come off' in the theatre, this was because he felt acutely conscious of operating outside his proper artistic *milieu*. But at his age *Hansel and Gretel* was an admirably gallant experiment – though one undertaken too late to influence his career.

The hard working day served him a little longer. He still longed to succeed in portraiture, and in 1934 received 250 guineas for a posthumous portrait of his former neighbour Sir Henry Royce of Rolls-Royce. His illustrations for *The Pied Piper* (1934) were thoroughly happy, and his drawings for *Peer Gynt* (1936) remarkably fresh and interesting (see page 143). Between them came Poe's *Tales of Mystery and Imagination* (1935), one of the few commissions that Rackham did not really enjoy. He contrived a touch or two of his old romantic poetry, but for the most part was concerned to match his illustrations to the macabre quality of the text. He told Marita Ross that he doubted whether he could do it. In the event he almost overdid it, and assured her 'that his pictures were now so horrible that he was beginning to frighten himself!' They are a revelation of the concealed power hinted in *Comus*, but the book is not one with which lovers of Rackham are tempted to linger.

In 1935 he tested the public's affection by holding another exhibition at the Leicester Galleries, this time chiefly of works from *Hans Andersen* and *The Compleat Angler*, but including some 'straight' landscapes. It was the first time he had exhibited there since 1919, and he was delighted to find himself welcomed back in the Sunday papers as 'A Great Illustrator' and 'The Goblin Master'. A high proportion of the drawings were sold, two of them to the Victoria and Albert Museum.

The exhibition may have solaced him for the marriage of his daughter in the same year, which he celebrated by a wry drawing of himself as a typical 'Rackham' tree with two affectionate birds on one of its branches and a nest on another. This drawing is the best answer to those who would invest Rackham's 'subjectivity' with an over-serious psychological significance. It reminds us again that he was

Design for act-drop of *Hansel and Gretel,* produced at the Cambridge Theatre, London, in 1933 (by courtesy of Peter Lazarus, Esq.).

fully aware of the joke and, on informal occasions, had been willing to contribute to it. Rackham enjoyed poking fun at himself – a sure sign of a healthy state of mind.

Philip Soper & Barbara Rackham were married on 27th July 1935 !

And they live at 6 Regent Square London W.C.1

When the American George Macy called on Rackham in the summer of 1936 at his ivy-covered, red-roofed cottage studio off Fitzroy Road, he, too, found him 'looking like a character out of one of his own drawings'. 'In the last years of his life, when I knew him,' wrote Macy in *The Horn Book* (May–June 1940), 'his head seemed always cocked to one side, bright and eager and smiling and cheerful; his cheeks were pink and bright; his eyes bright blue and clear; his emotions used his face as a field to play on.' Macy had called on behalf of the Limited Editions Club of New York to invite Rackham to illustrate James Stephens' *The Crock of Gold*. He found him, for

Peer and the Threadballs. *Peer Gynt,* 1936: George G. Harrap & Co. Ltd.

143

the first time for many years, at something of a loose end. Rackham soon agreed to tackle *The Crock of Gold*, but said that he would be glad to have another commission as well, so that he would know what he could turn to after his work for Stephens' book was finished.

The pair sat in the studio for a long while, talking vaguely of what he might do. In a desultory fashion, Macy eventually threw out the suggestion: 'What about *The Wind in the Willows*?'

Macy then saw Rackham much moved. 'Immediately a wave of emotion crossed his face; he gulped, started to say something, turned his back on me and went to the door for a few minutes.' When he came back he explained that for years he had ardently wished to illustrate the book, and had always regretted that he had refused the invitation of Kenneth Grahame and his publishers nearly thirty years before. He welcomed the opportunity offered him by Macy with open arms, insisting that he must illustrate *The Wind in the Willows* before *The Crock of Gold*. As he was determined to take his time, a contract was prepared by which Rackham agreed to deliver the drawings to the Limited Editions Club in the spring of 1938.

That Rackham's last subject in book-illustration (for so it proved) should have been one in which he took especial pleasure, and of which he made an outstanding success, demonstrates a kind of poetic justice not commonly found. 'It's a splendid book, isn't it!' he had written to the Simon children in 1909 (see pages 82–3). To him and countless others it had remained a splendid book; and it is now all the more splendid for later generations because its text can be read side by side with Rackham's entrancing river scenes and the most sympathetic studies of the small animals that he ever achieved. There is a mellow grace, a gentle wisdom, an affectionate humour in these drawings that make them the perfect farewell.

It is a strange paradox, but one revealing of the man and his character, that these last drawings should have been perhaps the

'It was a golden afternoon; the smell of the dust they kicked up was rich and satisfying.'
The Wind in the Willows, 1940 (by courtesy of Mrs Barbara Edwards).

gayest and happiest of all his illustrations; for the work was rendered most arduous for him, first by Mrs Rackham's increasingly serious illness, then by his own gradually failing health. But he began the task immediately: a letter from the author's widow, Mrs Kenneth Grahame, at Pangbourne, is dated 8th September 1936. In it Mrs Grahame says that she will be 'very glad' to help Rackham 'to discern the special spots on this reach of the river that might be connected with Toad, Mole and Company', and she continues:

'The trees which are such a feature along the river-bank here are really more full of "drawing" when the leaves are off – but you may not be able to wait for this aspect – or you may wish to see them (the trees) both in leaf & later on in branch. I know that Kenneth wrote to a small schoolgirl in an elementary school, who had written a prize essay on "The Wind in the Willows" – "I have always thought of 'Toad Hall' as being on the Oxfordshire side of the river" – & I know a house, Elizabethan but somewhat ornate, that might serve as a model. There is a lovely backwater where Mole & Rat may have boated, & a spit of foreshore where the swans nest, on which a year or two ago 2 baby otters were found. . . .

'I rather hope you may not be time-driven to come till the weather is better again – as at present it is too windy to go *on* the river – which you might wish to do.

'I shall be glad to help in any way in my power to show you the scenes & settings most appropriate to your purpose. . . .'

There was no hurry; Rackham's drawings show trees that are bare and trees that are in leaf; he took several walks beside the river with Mrs Grahame. By the spring of 1938, he could report only limited progress, however, and in the autumn of that year he went into the Oxted and Limpsfield Cottage Hospital for an operation for internal

' "Shove that under your feet," he observed to the Mole, as he passed it down into the boat.'
Rackham's last drawing, 1939. From *The Wind in the Willows* (by courtesy of Mrs Barbara
Edwards).

147

cancer. On 22nd November 1938, he wrote a pencilled note from the hospital to Mrs E. Williams Bailey, an admirer and collector of his work:

'I wish I could give a good account of either my wife or myself. My wife has borne up amid great disturbances astonishingly well, but I fear it cannot be said that she is better. And I – well the less said the better. Henceforth life will only be possible for me with the aid of a surgical nurse – whether at home or at the hospital as at present. I wish I could stop losing weight – but I eat with difficulty & haemorrhage is frequent & severe. So I am *very* weak.'

And on 28th November he wrote to the same correspondent:

'. . . I am told I must not expect to be able to gauge the future possibilities for my life in less than about a year. It turns on unknown conditions that cannot be got at – due to the capricious behaviour of a gland, that *may* get tired of its misbehaviour, or the reverse – in which case my difficulties will be very great. However, we must wait & see. My best hope is to feed as well as I can (at present a very poor effort) & never tire myself.'

He returned home to Stilegate with no illusions; his London studio was abandoned; and as time showed that he was not to recover he became very low and depressed. He spent much of the time in bed, but there were days when he still felt strong enough to work and deal with his affairs. In April 1939, Mary Truby King wrote to Heinemann from Adelaide, asking permission to use a drawing from Swinburne's *The Springtide of Life* – 'quite the most charming "natural feeding" picture I have seen' – as a frontispiece for her book *Mothercraft*, and added: 'I feel sure that Mr Arthur Rackham, or his trustees (I think he is dead, but am not sure) would not mind the picture being used for this purpose.' Rackham wrote on this letter, in ink, and in a firm hand, that he had agreed to the proposal for a fee of ten guineas and an appropriate acknowledgement.

In June an old friend, the poet and wood-engraver T. Sturge Moore, sent him a kindly letter full of gossip about mutual acquaintances of their student days, and telling him the latest news of the Art-Workers' Guild. 'I was very glad to learn that you enjoy respites from exhaustion sometimes long enough to let you get on with the work you have on hand,' wrote Sturge Moore; 'I hope you can enjoy the light and heat and that they will help you to stave off exhaustion.' It was a fine summer, and once, while he was lying in the garden, Rackham said to his nurse: 'How nice it would be if I could die here under the trees!'

Slowly, the drawings for *The Wind in the Willows* neared completion. The last drawing of all to be finished was that of Rat and Mole loading their boat for the picnic (see page 147). Rackham's daughter remembers his great exhaustion and the extreme difficulty he had in getting it done. When he had, as he thought, finished it, he suddenly discovered that there were no oars in the boat. Barbara tried to persuade him that this was a detail that did not matter, but he insisted that everything must be right, and with great labour he altered the drawing and put in the oars. After he had done this, he lay back in bed and said: 'Thank goodness, that is the last one.' And so it proved in every sense.

Arthur Rackham died on 6th September 1939, a few days before his seventy-second birthday. His ending, like his whole life and the strong clear strokes of his pen, had been gallant and true. He had finished his work, and he had made ready his boat for a journey.

CHAPTER EIGHT

Epilogue

NDER the shadow of the opening of the Second World War, Rackham's death received less attention in the Press than it would have done at another time. The obituary notice in *The Times* described him as 'one of the most eminent book illustrators of his day' with 'a special place in the hearts of children', and contrasted his belief in 'the sacrosanct quality of the text' with an 'unmistakable personal idiosyncrasy'. 'His genius had something of the Gothic flavour . . . his line was in the last degree sensitive.'

In December 1939, the memorial exhibition at the Leicester Galleries brought together examples of Rackham's finest work from his best period, together with several of his landscapes and the majority of the principal drawings for Poe's *Tales, Peer Gynt,* and *The Wind in the Willows.* The writer of the introductory note in the catalogue was excusably a partisan. He removed the guarded qualification of *The Times'* obituarist and made no bones about describing Arthur Rackham as 'the most eminent book illustrator of his day'.

The Wind in the Willows, with Rackham's last illustrations, was published in New York by the Limited Editions Club in 1940. On this volume Bruce Rogers, greatest of American book designers, lavished all his skill. The drawings were not generally known in

150

England until Methuen published a popular edition at a guinea in 1950, omitting a few of the plates, including the frontispiece in which Toad, disguised as a washerwoman, attempts to bargain with the booking-clerk at the railway station – a clerk who bears an unmistakable resemblance to Arthur Rackham. The Methuen volume received a warm recognition that was all the more spontaneous because the drawings came to most people as a complete surprise.

Rackham's will, drawn up in favour of his wife and daughter, was proved at nearly £25,000. Mrs Rackham did not long survive her husband. She died in March 1941, aged seventy-three.

As Rackham's death occurred in the early days of the war, it proved impossible to fulfil his wish for cremation at Golders Green because the undertakers, fearful of air raids that did not happen, refused to venture into London. His funeral therefore took place at Croydon. When Mrs Rackham died, heavy air raids were such everyday occurrences that no objections were raised. Edyth Rackham was cremated at Golders Green, and her ashes were then scattered with her husband's in the Garden of Remembrance there.

Since his death Rackham's prestige in the book-collectors' market has been fully maintained. It is understandable that such a prolific illustrator, who kept up a remarkably high standard of achievement over a very long period, should have become a focus of interest.

The series of *de-luxe* signed editions, originally published at two or three guineas, sold consistently well on publication and have appreciated considerably in value amongst collectors. Current prices (1960) range from £5 to £30 according to scarcity and popularity; there were, for example, only 250 copies of the first of the series, *Rip Van Winkle* in 1905, while 1100 copies of the *de-luxe Alice* were issued in 1907 (the average size of the signed editions was about 500 copies). Although prices have inevitably fluctuated according to the changing economic situation, the general trend has been upward, and these handsome books have always found favour.

There is, however, plenty of opportunity for the Rackham collector outside this expensive field. Apart from the *de-luxe* series, there are the unlimited editions of the same works, of which the first impressions, sought by collectors, have also appreciated in value in similar proportions; and there are many other books illustrated by Rackham which were never issued in special limited editions. Then there are books including illustrations by Rackham amongst others by different artists; these may often be found by assiduous searchers, to their advantage, lurking unsuspected on bookshop shelves.

The enthusiast who cares to go even further can look for the many periodicals published during Rackham's early professional years which contain his illustrations for stories and articles, sometimes in his characteristic manner and sometimes far from it. In journals from *Little Folks* to *The Ladies' Field* his fine line may be recognized. Often his initials identify the work, but the drawings are not always signed, and a need for detective ingenuity creeps in when one encounters the initials of another 'A.R.' who was a block-maker and not an illustrator.

Altogether, the hunt for books illustrated by Rackham has already provided much pleasure for those who are disposed to take it up, and may well provide a great deal more, whatever the current prices may happen to be (and they will always vary according to the circumstances of a sale and the condition of the book). It might be mentioned that the *Peter Pan Portfolio* (1912), containing twelve enlarged plates of illustrations in the 1906 *Peter Pan in Kensington Gardens*, is something of a freak in the Rackham bibliography. High prices have been paid for it, because it is scarce, and because the plates can be resold separately, but the *Portfolio* is a law unto itself and no reliable guide to the Rackham market.

These *Peter Pan* prints should perhaps rank with Rackham's

original drawings as examples of his decorative work, rather than with his books. Rackham is one of the few English illustrators whose originals have sold readily. When he wrote a note to accompany his will, in 1934, concerning the relatively small number of his drawings still in his possession, Rackham was depressed at the state of the art market. 'But the better drawings may well find buyers by degrees,' he said, 'the smaller ones not infrequently to book-collectors, rather than picture-buyers. For some years, I have found that a nett price of about £50 as an average (say from £30 to £60 – rarely more) is a possible price for the more important drawings, while smaller and less important drawings are sold at £15 to £30.' This position had not materially altered in 1960.

Rackham has had many imitators; but they have lacked his *finesse* and imaginative power; he remains unique. Max Reinhardt admitted his debt to Rackham's *Midsummer-Night's Dream* drawings in his production of the play, and, whether or not Rackham can be proved to have influenced Walt Disney – as, considering Rackham's American popularity, seems most likely – he undoubtedly anticipated his work. What of his effect on more serious artists? The influence of Rackham was felt most deeply in England by children who grew up during the first quarter of this century in those upper- and middle-class homes where his books were chiefly treasured. Two such sons of professional men were Graham Sutherland and John Piper, both born in 1903 and both educated at Epsom College. In this connection Sutherland's pre-occupation with trees and their roots could be significant; one could see it as part of the general subconscious influence of Rackham's art which has remained with all who knew it as children.

It would be idle to deny that Rackham has detractors, who fail to distinguish between the Master and his imitators and competitors, who mock at 'Fairies-at-the-bottom-of-the-garden', and who associate him, most unfairly, with terracotta gnomes outside seaside

u

153

bungalows. This prejudice cannot, it is submitted, survive an acquaintance with the width and range of his accomplishment, as demonstrated, however imperfectly, between the covers of this book.

That he has suffered from the diminishing acceptance of fairies in a disillusioned world is obvious. To those who consider them to be as imperishable and as necessary as folk-lore itself, Rackham is a valiant figure, for he, more than anyone, has kept the fairy world alive for children in the twentieth century. In an interview with James Milne (*The Book Monthly*, 1918–19), Rackham admitted that he saw fairy tales as 'general truths, rather than particular truths. True to human nature and human ways of considering human experience, sifted and transmuted till they become truer than truth, essence'. He had 'no use for the flimsy representation of spiritual realities'. Whether an artist believed in his fairy or not, Rackham knew that 'he must make it as real as if he did', as real as the tree the fairy is sitting on, or the mist around the tree.

If Rackham's fairies dance lightly out of the range of criticism, this does not mean that all his work is beyond criticism; we find heroic mythological figures who would obviously have been at home in the Edwardian Academy, and we find a degree of archness here and there among the Arcadian idylls; the humour of long noses can be exaggerated. But where much is offered, much can be forgiven. Rackham's work, though part of its strength is in detail, has a Shakespearean breadth and truth to nature. We know without being told, what is the fact – that this artist was a great reader, especially of the English classics; that for a Londoner, his knowledge of natural history was extensive and peculiar; that he observed the whole world of nature as a practising artist, with a sketch-book in his pocket.

Though Rackham sometimes appears to tread the verge of caricature, he was too gentle in himself, and too poetic, to make a caricaturist. His sphere is rather that of the lovable grotesque; A. S. Hartrick has seen him as the descendant of the English Medieval mural painters who decorated our country churches and brought a touch of humour to the portrayal of the 'Harrowings of Hell' and the Seven Deadly Sins. There is a famous cartoon by Raemakers, of the 1914–18 War, which shows figures representing the Allies cutting down a tree bearing the anguished features of the Kaiser. This political comment would have been too direct for Rackham. His personified trees (e.g. see pages 8 and 99) humorously suggest the mysteries of nature rather than any criticism of humanity. They are conceived in the spirit of T. E. Hulme's lines:

> *'With a courtly bow the bent tree sighed,*
> *May I present you to my friend the sun?'*

Rackham was a craftsman through and through. It is significant that a scrapbook that he kept in his last years contains cuttings of an article 'Back to Workmanship' by C. E. Montague, and of a report of a lecture by Charles Morgan, 'A Defence of Story-Telling'. He was a vigorous and perhaps too stubborn advocate of water-colour. But then, as he once wrote in an article,* 'From the first day when I was given, as all little boys are, a shilling paint-box . . . from that day, when I first put my water-colour brush in my mouth, and was told I mustn't, this craft has been my constant companion. . . . Looking back I have one long memory of holidays and never one without my faithful friend.'

Would the application of psychological analysis assist our appreciation of Rackham's drawings? A correspondent has told the present writer, in an interesting letter, that he believed Rackham's future standing would be high and that it would be based on the 'symbolic content' of his work as well as on its artistic merit. Whether this would be a fruitful approach to the work of a busy illustrator continually employed on commissioned subjects, not all of his own

---

* In *The Old Water-Colour Society's Club Eleventh Annual Volume*, 1934.

choosing, may be thought doubtful. It is one thing to demonstrate the symbolism of a fairy-tale, which may plausibly be done, and another thing to use that information to psycho-analyse the illustrator. As a man's character is always reflected in his work, we must be aware that Rackham's sensitivity and the sweep of his imagination were both unusual. This biographical sketch presents the cheerful, methodical artist whom 'all men knew', but allows the psychologists to have their say elsewhere.

In assessing Rackham's place as an illustrator, there is no need to make extravagant claims, no need to match him against the great Victorians (though it might be mentioned that his subject-matter was healthier than Beardsley's and his imaginative range wider than Tenniel's). Despite the German influences, Rackham's work remained utterly English in spirit. Succeeding and supplanting Randolph Caldecott, Kate Greenaway and Walter Crane, Rackham possessed the ability and the thoroughness required to make the most of the new methods of reproduction that became available to him, and the genius to make his drawings immediately distinctive and worthwhile – as effective, indeed, on the walls of a room as between the covers of a book. His reward has been not only a world-wide reputation but the affection felt by a multitude, young and old, for the 'Beloved Enchanter', 'Le Peintre-Sorcier'.

Appendixes

Silhouette chapter-head from *The Wind in the Willows*.

A decorative drawing which suggests the influence of Beardsley: endpaper design for *Shooting*, 1902 (the Haddon Hall Library Edition).

APPENDIX A

Bibliography

WORKS CONSULTED FOR THE BIOGRAPHY

The Studio, 15th April 1905: 'Arthur Rackham: A Painter of Fantasies', by A. L. Baldry.

The Girl's Realm, November 1908: 'English Illustrators of Juvenile Books', by Haldane Macfall.

The Sphere, 27th November 1909: 'The Art-Book Cult of the Season: The Work of Arthur Rackham'.

Dekorative Kunst (Munich), December 1909: 'Arthur Rackham', by Ethel M. Chadwick.

Le Journal (Paris), 4th December 1911: 'Le Peintre-Sorcier'.

Art et Décoration (Paris), July 1912: 'Un Illustrateur Anglais: Arthur Rackham', by A. Marguillier.

St Nicholas (New York), March 1914: 'Arthur Rackham: The Wizard at Home', by Eleanor Farjeon.

The Book Monthly, Christmas 1918–New Year 1919: 'Mr Rackham and Fairies', by James Milne.

Arthur Rackham: A List of Books Illustrated by Him. Compiled by Frederick Coykendall, with an Introductory Note by Martin Birnbaum. New York, privately printed, 1922.

The Bookman, October 1925: 'The Worst Time in My Life', by Arthur Rackham.

The Bookman, October 1926: 'The Value of Criticism', by Arthur Rackham.

The Bookman, December 1933: 'Some Earlier Illustrated Books of Arthur Rackham', by E. A. Osborne.

The Old Water-Colour Society's Club, Eleventh Annual Volume, 1934: 'In Praise of Water-Colour', by Arthur Rackham.

The Art-Workers' Guild: 1884–1934, by H. J. L. J. Massé, 1935.

Arthur Rackham: A Bibliography, by Sarah Briggs Latimore and Grace Clark Haskell. Los Angeles, 1936.

The Horn Book Magazine (Boston, U.S.A.), November–December 1939: 'The Three Owls' Notebook: A Christmas Ride with Arthur Rackham', by Anne Carroll Moore.

The Horn Book Magazine (Boston, U.S.A.), May–June 1940: 'The Genius of Arthur

BIBLIOGRAPHY

Rackham', by Robert Lawson; 'Arthur Rackham and *The Wind in the Willows*', by George Macy; 'The Home of the Wee Folk: Where Arthur Rackham Lived and Worked in the Heart of Sussex Downs', by P. G. Konody.

The Old Water-Colour Society's Club Eighteenth Annual Volume, 1940. 'Arthur Rackham: An Appreciation', by A. S. Hartrick, R.W.S.

Dictionary of National Biography, 1931–40. Arthur Rackham, by Herbert B. Grimsditch.

Everybody's Weekly, 27th September 1947: 'The Beloved Enchanter', by Marita Ross.

Other contemporary magazines and newspapers;

catalogues of the Leicester Galleries, London:

the books illustrated by Arthur Rackham.

APPENDIX B

Drawings and Paintings
in Collections

SOME DRAWINGS AND PAINTINGS BY ARTHUR RACKHAM IN PUBLIC AND SEMI-PUBLIC COLLECTIONS

In water-colour, or pen-and-ink and water-colour, unless otherwise stated. All small-scale, except the self-portrait

LONDON

Art-Workers' Guild. Queen Square
Self-portrait, 1924. Oils.

Tate Gallery, Millbank
'The Dance in Cupid's Alley.' 1904. Based on a poem by Austin Dobson: 'O, Love's but a dance', etc.

Victoria and Albert Museum
'The Widow Whitgift and her Sons.' From *Puck of Pook's Hill*. 1906.
'To hear the sea-maid's music.' From *A Midsummer-Night's Dream*, II, i. 1908.

Headpiece to *The Ring of the Nibelungs*, Vol. I, *The Rhinegold – The Valkyrie*. 1910.
'South Downs at Amberley.' 1926.
'Isaak Walton reclining against a Fence.' From *The Compleat Angler*. 1931.

BEVERLEY, YORKSHIRE

Art Gallery
Two drawings for *Gulliver's Travels*.

BRADFORD

Art Gallery
'The Magic Carpet.' Acquired 1907.

DRAWINGS AND PAINTINGS

CAMBRIDGE

Fitzwilliam Museum
'Blythburgh, Suffolk.' Pencil and water-colour.
'The Trees and the Axe.' From *Aesop's Fables*, 1912.

HARROGATE

Art Gallery
'Regent's Park.' 1928.

NOTTINGHAM

Museum and Art Gallery
'It amused the birds to see him lifting the crusts to his mouth with hands.' For *Peter Pan in Kensington Gardens*.

PRESTON

Harris Museum and Art Gallery
'Jewels from the Deep.' 1909.
'Bigbury Bay, Devon.' 1915.

SHREWSBURY SCHOOL

Moser Collection
'Snowstorm: Montana.' 1914.

FOREIGN COLLECTIONS

BARCELONA

Municipal Gallery
'Imps of the Smoke.' Acquired 1911.

CAMBRIDGE, MASS.

Harvard University Library
The Houghton Library has drawings for *Little Brother and Little Sister, English Fairy Tales*, and *Aesop's Fables*, also an unidentified drawing 'Grotesque Sprites'.

MELBOURNE

National Gallery
'Windfalls.' 1904.

NEW YORK

Butler Library, Columbia University
Sarah Briggs Latimore's comprehensive collection of books and drawings was acquired by Mr and Mrs Alfred C. Berol for presentation to Columbia University, and a selection was exhibited there, December 1956–March 1957. The drawings, about sixty in number, in pencil, pen-and-ink, water-colour, etc., include examples of illustrations for *Gulliver's Travels, Rip Van Winkle, Mother Goose, Aesop's Fables, Comus, Undine*, and *A Legend of Sleepy Hollow*, and a series for *The Lonesomest Doll*. This was followed by an even more important addition in 1958 of some three hundred original drawings and sketches, together with about thirty volumes of the artist's sketchbooks in which his major illustrated books were planned. Another Rackham Collection, brought together by Grace Clark Haskell, is in the Free Library of Philadelphia.

Public Library
The Spencer Collection has twenty-one original drawings in water-colour for seventeen books published between 1906

and 1921, from *Peter Pan in Kensington Gardens* to *A Dish of Apples*. The Spencer Collection also possesses Rackham's illustrations and decorations for the MS of *A Midsummer-Night's Dream* written out by Graily Hewitt, comprising thirteen full-page water-colour drawings, three full-page borders in colour, vignettes and head and tail-pieces. The illustrations differ from those in the book published in 1908.

Musée National d'Art Moderne (Edmund Davis Collection). 'Jack Sprat and his Wife.' 1912. Presented 1915.

Gallery of Drawings and Water-Colour Paintings. 'The Footbridge.' Acquired 1912.

APPENDIX C

The Printed Work of Arthur Rackham

A CHECK-LIST COMPILED BY

BERTRAM ROTA

PRINTED WORK

THIS CHECK-LIST is based upon the bibliographical notes on Arthur Rackham's books compiled by E. A. Osborne (published serially in *The Book Trade Journal*, London, in 1936), the full-length bibliography of Rackham's books, periodical contributions, etc., by Sarah Briggs Latimore and Grace Clark Haskell (published in a limited edition by Suttonhouse, Los Angeles, in 1936) and the extensive collection formed by Mr George Lazarus (which includes many previously unrecorded items).

The compiler of this check-list gratefully acknowledges his indebtedness to the pioneer work of those enthusiasts, and refers all who seek fuller information about the original printings to the Latimore-Haskell bibliography, now out of print but available in many reference libraries.

It cannot be hoped that the present list is complete, especially in its record of periodical contributions, but it is believed to include all the printed work of Arthur Rackham which has been traced through wide searches by several hands over many years and with the benefit of access to the artist's own records during his lifetime.

This check-list records the first printings and important new editions. Unless otherwise stated the place of publication is London. The numbers of illustrations given for the books illustrated wholly by Arthur Rackham refer to coloured, tinted or black-and-white illustrations, either full-page or in the text, but do not include minor decorations or designs for end-papers, covers and dust-wrappers.

Books illustrated wholly by Arthur Rackham

1894

HOPE, ANTHONY: *The Dolly Dialogues.* Westminster Gazette. 4 illustrations.

1896

ADAIR-FITZGERALD, S. J.: *The Zankiwank and the Bletherwitch.* J. M. Dent & Co. 41 illustrations. (Also E. P. Dutton & Co., New York.)

MERRIMAN, HENRY SETON and TALLANTYRE, S. G.: *The Money-Spinner and other character notes.* Smith, Elder & Co. 12 illustrations.

1897

MERRIMAN, HENRY SETON: *The Grey Lady.* Smith, Elder & Co. 12 illustrations.

LEVER, CHARLES: *Charles O'Malley, the Irish Dragoon.* Service & Paton. 16 illustrations. (Also E. P. Putnam's Sons, New York.)

BROWNE, MAGGIE: *Two Old Ladies, Two Foolish Fairies and a Tom Cat. The Surprising Adventures of Tuppy and Tue.* Cassell & Co., Ltd. 23 illustrations. (Republished in 1904 as *The Surprising Adventures of Tuppy and Tue.*)

1898

BURNEY, FRANCES: *Evelina or The History of a Young Lady's Entrance into the World.* Geo. Newnes, Ltd. 16 illustrations.

[BARHAM, R. H.]: *The Ingoldsby Legends or Mirth and Marvels.* J. M. Dent & Co. 102 illustrations. (Republished in 1907 with revised illustrations.)

1899

MARTINEAU, HARRIET: *Feats on the Fjord, a tale.* J. M. Dent & Co.; *The Temple Classics for Young People.* 12 illustrations. (Republished in 1914 by J. M. Dent & Sons, Ltd with eight of these illustrations coloured by W. Cubitt Cooke.)

LAMB, CHARLES and MARY: *Tales from Shakespeare.* J. M. Dent & Co.; *The Temple Classics for Young People.* 12 illustrations. (Republished in 1909 with additional illustrations.)

1900

SWIFT, JONATHAN: *Gulliver's Travels into Several Remote Nations of the World.* J. M. Dent & Co.; *The Temple Classics for Young People.* 12 illustrations. (Republished in 1909 with additional illustrations.)

GRIMM, THE BROTHERS: *Fairy Tales.* A new translation by Mrs Edgar Lucas. Freemantle & Co. 100 illustrations. (Part of this edition was taken over and reissued by Constable & Co. and some copies were issued later with the imprint of Selfridge & Co. A new edition with only twelve of these illustrations was published by Partridge & Co. The work was republished in 1909 with additional illustrations.)

HERBERTSON, AGNES GROZIER: *The Bee-Blowaways*. Cassell & Co., Ltd. 17 illustrations. (One of the series of *Little Folks Panel Books*.)

1901

KENYON, C. R.: *The Argonauts of the Amazon*. W. & R. Chambers, Ltd. 6 illustrations. (Also published by E. P. Dutton & Co., New York.)

1903

NIEBUHR: *The Greek Heroes, stories translated from Niebuhr, with additions*. Cassell & Co., Ltd. 12 illustrations.

HENTY, G. A., and OTHERS: *Brains and Bravery*, being stories told by G. A. Henty, Guy Boothby, L. T. Meade, J. Arthur Barry, Katharine Tynan, H. A. Bryden and others. 8 illustrations.

GREENE, THE HON. MRS: *The Grey House on the Hill*. Thomas Nelson & Sons. 8 illustrations.

1904

CHOLMONDELEY, MARY: *Red Pottage*. Geo. Newnes, Ltd. 8 illustrations. (One of the *Newnes' Sixpenny Novels Illustrated* series.)

BROWNE, MAGGIE: *The Surprising Adventures of Tuppy and Tue*. Cassell & Co., Ltd. 23 illustrations. (A reprint under a new title of *Two Old Ladies, Two Foolish Fairies and a Tom Cat*, published in 1897.)

DRURY, MAJOR W. P.: *The Peradventures of Private Paget*. Chapman & Hall, Ltd. 8 illustrations.

HARBOUR, HENRY: *Where Flies the Flag*. Collins' Clear-Type Press. 6 illustrations.

DANA, RICHARD HENRY: *Two Years Before the Mast*. Collins' Clear-Type Press. 8 illustrations. (Also published by The John C. Winston Co., New York.)

1905

IRVING, WASHINGTON: *Rip Van Winkle*. William Heinemann. 51 illustrations. (There was also a *de-luxe* issue limited to 250 copies signed by Rackham. Also published by Doubleday, Page & Co., New York, in a trade edition.)

HAYDON, A. L.: *Stories of King Arthur*. Cassell & Co., Ltd; *Book 5 of Cassell's Fairy Tale Series*. 6 illustrations. (This booklet was reissued by Cassell's, later in the same year, bound up with four others, under the general title of *Fairy Tales Old and New*.)

1906

BARRIE, J. M.: *Peter Pan in Kensington Gardens*. Hodder & Stoughton. 50 illustrations. (There was also a *de-luxe* issue limited to 500 copies signed by Rackham. Also published by Charles Scribner's Sons, New York, in a trade edition.) A new edition was published in 1912 with a new coloured frontispiece, seven additional full-page illustrations, a new cover design, etc. There was also a *de-luxe* issue of this new edition, bound in vellum. Twelve of the coloured plates for the 1906 edition were issued, much enlarged, as *The Peter Pan Portfolio* in 1912. The edition was to be limited to 600 sets, of which it was intended that the first 100 should have each plate signed by the artist. In fact only about 20 sets were so signed. An American edition of the same twelve plates, limited to 300 sets, was published by Brentano's in New York in 1914. Some of Rackham's illustrations for *Peter Pan* were used, reduced in size, for an edition *retold for little people* and published in 1930.

KIPLING, RUDYARD: *Puck of Pook's Hill*. Doubleday, Page & Co., New York. 4 illustrations. (Rackham's illustrations for this book were not published in England.)

1907

CARROLL, LEWIS: *Alice's Adventures in Wonderland*. William Heinemann. 27 illustrations. (There was also a *de-luxe* edition limited to 1,130 copies. Also published by Doubleday, Page & Co., New York, in a trade edition and in a *de-luxe* edition limited to 550 copies.)

[BONSER, A. E., WOOLF, B. SIDNEY, and BUCHLEIM, E. S.]: *The Land of Enchantment*. Cassell & Co., Ltd. 37 illustrations. (Five stories by three authors, which originally appeared in *Little Folks* magazine between 1896 and 1902.)

GATES, ELEANOR: *Good Night*. Thomas Y. Crowell Co., New York. 5 illustrations. (There was no English edition of this book.)

[BARHAM, R. H.]: *The Ingoldsby Legends or Mirth and Marvels*. J. M. Dent & Co. 102 illustrations. (There was also a *de-luxe* edition limited to 560 copies signed by Rackham, of which 50 were reserved for U.S.A. Also published by E. P. Dutton & Co., New York, in a trade edition.) This is a revised edition of the work originally published in 1898, with some new illustrations substituted and others redrawn and recoloured.

1908

SHAKESPEARE, WILLIAM: *A Midsummer-Night's Dream*. William Heinemann. 70 illustrations. (There was also a *de-luxe* edition limited to 1,000 copies signed by Rackham. Also published by Doubleday, Page & Co., New York, in a trade edition.)

1909

SWIFT, JONATHAN: *Gulliver's Travels into Several Remote Nations of the World*. J. M. Dent & Co. 14 illustrations. (There was also a *de-luxe* edition limited to 750 copies signed by Rackham and with an extra plate. Also published by E. P. Dutton & Co., New York, in a trade edition.) This is a revised edition of the work originally published in 1900, with some additional illustrations and others redrawn and coloured.

LAMB, CHARLES and MARY: *Tales from Shakespeare*. J. M. Dent & Co. 14 illustrations. (There was also a *de-luxe* edition limited to 750 copies signed by Rackham with an extra plate. Also published by E. P. Dutton & Co., New York, in a trade edition.) This is a revised edition of the work originally published in 1899, with some additional illustrations and others redrawn and coloured.

GRIMM, THE BROTHERS: *Fairy Tales*. Constable & Co., Ltd. 95 illustrations. (There was also a *de-luxe* edition limited to 750 copies signed by Rackham. Also published in New York in a trade edition.) This is a revised edition of the work originally published in 1900, with some new illustrations and others redrawn and coloured.

FOUQUE, DE LA MOTTE: *Undine*. Adapted from the German by W. L. Courteney. William Heinemann. 45 illustrations. (There was also a *de-luxe* edition limited to 1,000 copies signed by Rackham. Also published by Doubleday, Page & Co., New York, in a trade edition and a *de-luxe* edition limited to 250 copies signed by Rackham.)

1910

BROWNE, MAGGIE: *The Book of Betty Barber*. Duckworth & Co. 18 illustrations.

WAGNER, RICHARD: *The Rhinegold and the Valkyrie*. William Heinemann. 48 illustrations. (There was also a *de-luxe* edition limited to 1,150 copies signed by Rackham, of which 150 were reserved for U.S.A. Also published by Doubleday, Page & Co., New York, in a trade edition.)

1911

WAGNER, RICHARD: *Siegfried and The Twilight of the Gods*. William Heinemann. 39 illustrations. (There was also a *de-luxe* edition limited to 1,150 copies signed by Rackham, of which 150 were reserved for U.S.A. Also published by Doubleday, Page & Co., New York, in a trade edition.)

1912

AESOP: *Aesop's Fables*. William Heinemann. 65 illustrations. (There was also a *de-luxe* edition limited to 1,450 copies signed by Rackham, of which 250 were reserved for U.S.A. and 200 for Australia. Also published by Doubleday, Page & Co., New York, in a trade edition.)

BARRIE, J. M.: *Peter Pan in Kensington Gardens*. New edition. Hodder & Stoughton, Ltd. 62 illustrations. (See under 1906: BARRIE.)

The Peter Pan Portfolio: Hodder & Stoughton, Ltd. 12 plates. (See under 1906: BARRIE.)

1913

Mother Goose. The Old Nursery Rhymes. William Heinemann. 98 illustrations. (There was also a *de-luxe* edition limited to 1,130 copies, signed by Rackham. Also published in New York, in a trade edition, with 79 illustrations and an additional title-page design in colour.)

Arthur Rackham's Book of Pictures. William Heinemann. 54 illustrations. (There was also a *de-luxe* edition limited to 1,030 copies signed by Rackham. Also published by The Century Co., New York, in a trade edition.)

1915

DICKENS, CHARLES: *A Christmas Carol*. William Heinemann. 32 illustrations. (There was also a *de-luxe* edition limited to 530 copies signed by Rackham. Also published by J. B. Lippincott Co., Philadelphia, in a trade edition and a *de-luxe* edition limited to 100 copies signed by Rackham. Republished in 1916 by William Heinemann, London, and Doubleday, Page & Co., New York, with 38 illustrations, some new.)

1916

The Allies' Fairy Book. William Heinemann. 36 illustrations. (There was also a *de-luxe* edition limited to 525 copies signed by Rackham. Also published by J. B. Lippincott Co., Philadelphia, in a trade edition and a *de-luxe* limited edition.)

1917

GRIMM, THE BROTHERS: *Little Brother and Little Sister*. Constable & Co., Ltd. 55 illustrations. (There was also a *de-luxe* edition limited to 525 copies signed by Rackham, with an extra plate. Also published by Dodd, Mead & Co., New York, in a trade edition.)

MALORY, SIR THOMAS: *The Romance of King Arthur and his Knights of the Round Table*. Abridged from Malory's *Morte D'Arthur* by Alfred Pollard. Macmillan & Co., Ltd. 86 illustrations. (There was also a *de-luxe* edition limited to 500 copies signed by Rackham. Also published by The Macmillan Co., New York, in a trade edition and a *de-luxe* edition limited to 250 copies, unsigned.)

1918

STEEL, FLORA ANNIE: *English Fairy Tales Retold*. Macmillan & Co., Ltd. 57 illustrations. (There was also a *de-luxe* edition limited to 500 copies signed by Rackham. Also published by The Macmillan Co., New York, in a trade edition.)

SWINBURNE, ALGERNON CHARLES: *The Springtide of Life; poems of childhood*. William Heinemann. 60 illustrations. (There was also a *de-luxe* edition with an extra plate, limited to 765 copies signed by Rackham, of which 100 copies were reserved for U.S.A. Also published by J. B. Lippincott Co., Philadelphia, in a trade edition.)

1919

Cinderella. Retold by C. S. Evans. William Heinemann. 53 illustrations. (There was also a *de-luxe* edition with an extra plate, limited to 525 copies on hand-made paper and 325 on Japanese vellum. Also published by J. B. Lippincott Co., Philadelphia, in a trade edition.)

FORD, JULIA ELLSWORTH: *Snickerty Nick, Rhymes by Whitter Bynner*. Moffat, Yard & Co., New York. 13 illustrations. (There was no English edition of the children's play. Eleven of these illustrations were reprinted in a new edition published by Suttonhouse, Los Angeles and San Francisco, with music, in 1935.)

Some British Ballads. Constable & Co., Ltd. 40 illustrations. (There was also a *de-luxe* edition limited to 575 copies signed by

Rackham. Also published by Dodd, Mead & Co., New York, in a trade edition.) This book was transferred to Heinemann in 1919 and issued with an inserted leaf announcing the change of publisher. This leaf bears a small new decoration by Rackham.

1920

The Sleeping Beauty. Retold by C. S. Evans. William Heinemann. 40 illustrations. (There was also a *de-luxe* edition with an extra plate, limited to 625 copies signed by Rackham, of which 100 were reserved for U.S.A. Also published by J. B. Lippincott Co., Philadelphia, in a trade edition.)

STEPHENS, JAMES: *Irish Fairy Tales*. Macmillan & Co., Ltd. 37 illustrations. (There was also a *de-luxe* edition limited to 520 copies signed by Rackham. Also published by The Macmillan Co., New York, in a trade edition.)

GRIMM, THE BROTHERS: *Snowdrop and Other Tales*. Constable & Co., Ltd. 49 illustrations. (This is a reprint, under a new title but with the same illustrations, of twenty-five stories previously published in *The Fairy Tales of the Brothers Grimm* in 1909. Also published by E. P. Dutton & Co., New York.)

GRIMM, THE BROTHERS: *Hansel and Gretel and Other Tales*. Constable & Co., Ltd. 48 illustrations. (This is a reprint, under a new title but with the same illustrations, of thirty stories previously published in *The Fairy Tales of the Brothers Grimm* in 1909. Also published by E. P. Dutton & Co., New York.)

1921

PHILLPOTTS, EDEN: *A Dish of Apples*. Hodder & Stoughton, Ltd. 26 illustrations. (There was also a *de-luxe* edition limited to 500 copies signed by Rackham.)

MILTON, JOHN: *Comus*. William Heinemann. 61 illustrations. (There was also a *de-luxe* edition limited to 530 copies signed by Rackham, of which 100 were reserved for U.S.A. Also published by Doubleday, Page & Co., New York, in a trade edition.)

1922

HAWTHORNE, NATHANIEL: *A Wonder Book*. Hodder & Stoughton, Ltd. 44 illustrations. (There was also a *de-luxe* edition limited to 600 copies signed by Rackham. Also published by George H. Doran Co., New York, in a trade edition.)

1923

A Fairy Book. Doubleday, Page & Co., New York. 31 illustrations. (This is a reprint, under a new title but with only 31 of the original illustrations, of the book previously published as *The Allies' Fairy Book* in 1916.)

1925

MORLEY, CHRISTOPHER: *Where the Blue Begins*. William Heinemann, Ltd. 20 illustrations. (There was also a *de-luxe* edition limited to 175 copies signed by Rackham. Also published by Doubleday, Page & Co., New York, in a trade edition and a *de-luxe* edition limited to 100 copies signed by Morley and Rackham.) This is an illustrated reprint of a book originally published without illustrations in 1922. Only the original copyright date is given on the reverse of the title-page.

BIANCO, MARGERY WILLIAMS: *Poor Cecco*. George H. Doran Co. 31 illustrations. (There was also a *de-luxe* edition limited to 105 copies signed by the author. Also published by Chatto & Windus, London, in a trade edition.)

1926

SHAKESPEARE, WILLIAM: *The Tempest*. (William Heinemann, Ltd. 45 illustrations. (There was also a *de-luxe* edition, with an extra plate, limited to 560 copies signed by Rackham, of which 260 copies were reserved for U.S.A. Also published by Doubleday, Page & Co., New York, in a trade edition.)

1928

BROWN, ABBIE FARWELL: *The Lonesomest Doll*. Houghton Mifflin Co., Boston and New York. 30 illustrations. (This is a new illustrated edition of a book originally published in 1901 with illustrations by a different artist. There was no English edition.)

IRVING, WASHINGTON: *The Legend of Sleepy Hollow*. George G. Harrap & Co., Ltd. 38 illustrations. (There was also a *de-luxe* edition limited to 375 copies signed by Rackham, of which 125 copies were reserved for U.S.A. Also published by David McKay Co., Philadelphia, in a trade edition.)

1929

GOLDSMITH, OLIVER: *The Vicar of Wakefield*. George G. Harrap & Co., Ltd. 34 illustrations. (There was also a *de-luxe* edition limited to 775 copies signed by Rackham, of which 200 copies were reserved for U.S.A. Also published by David McKay Co., Philadelphia, in a trade edition.)

1930

BYRON, MAY: *J. M. Barrie's Peter Pan in Kensington Gardens retold for little people*. Hodder & Stoughton, Ltd. 20 illustrations. (These illustrations are reprinted, reduced in size, from the 1906 and 1912 editions. Also published by Charles Scribner's Sons, New York.)

1931

WALTON, IZAAK: *The Compleat Angler.* George G. Harrap & Co., Ltd. 37 illustrations. (There was also a *de-luxe* edition limited to 775 copies signed by Rackham. Also published by David McKay Co., Philadelphia, in a trade edition.)

MOORE, CLEMENT C.: *The Night Before Christmas.* George G. Harrap & Co., Ltd. 21 illustrations. (There was also a *de-luxe* edition limited to 550 copies signed by Rackham, of which 275 copies were reserved for U.S.A. Also published by J. B. Lippincott Co., Philadelphia, in a trade edition.)

DICKENS, CHARLES: *The Chimes.* The Limited Editions Club, New York. 20 illustrations. (Only published in this edition limited to 1,500 copies signed by Rackham.)

1932

RUSKIN, JOHN: *The King of the Golden River.* George G. Harrap & Co., Ltd. 19 illustrations. (There was also a *de-luxe* edition limited to 570 copies signed by Rackham. Also published by J. B. Lippincott Co., Philadelphia, in a trade edition.)

ANDERSEN, HANS: *Fairy Tales.* George G. Harrap & Co., Ltd. 71 illustrations. (There was also a *de-luxe* edition limited to 525 copies signed by Rackham. Also published by David McKay Co., Philadelphia, in a trade edition.)

1933

ROSSETTI, CHRISTINA: *Goblin Market.* George G. Harrap & Co., Ltd. 23 illustra-

tions. (There was also a *de-luxe* edition limited to 410 copies signed by Rackham. Also published by J. B. Lippincott Co., Philadelphia, in a trade edition.)

The Arthur Rackham Fairy Book. George G. Harrap & Co., Ltd. 68 illustrations. (There was also a *de-luxe* edition limited to 460 copies signed by Rackham. Also published by J. B. Lippincott Co., Philadelphia, in a trade edition.)

1934

BROWNING, ROBERT: *The Pied Piper of Hamelin.* George G. Harrap & Co., Ltd. 18 illustrations. (There was also a *de-luxe* edition limited to 410 copies signed by Rackham. Also published by J. B. Lippincott Co., Philadelphia, in a trade edition.)

1935

POE, EDGAR ALLEN: *Tales of Mystery and Imagination.* George G. Harrap & Co., Ltd. 40 illustrations. (There was also a *de-luxe* edition limited to 460 copies signed by Rackham. Also published by J. B. Lippincott Co., Philadelphia in a trade edition.)

1936

IBSEN, HENRIK: *Peer Gynt.* George G. Harrap & Co., Ltd. 19 illustrations. (There was also a *de-luxe* edition limited to 450 copies signed by Rackham. Also published by J. B. Lippincott Co., Philadelphia, in a trade edition.)

1939

SHAKESPEARE, WILLIAM: *A Midsummer-Night's Dream.* The Limited Editions Club, New York. 6 illustrations. (Limited to 1,950 copies.) This is one of the 37 volumes of the set of Shakespeare's works, each illustrated by a different artist, produced for members of the Limited Editions Club in 1939–40. The illustrations are not those used in Heinemann's edition of 1908.

1940

GRAHAME, KENNETH: *The Wind in the Willows*. The Limited Editions Club, New York. 16 illustrations. (Limited to 2,020 copies signed by Bruce Rogers. Also published by The Heritage Press, New York, in a trade edition. The first English edition to incorporate these illustrations was published in 1950 by Methuen, who in the following year issued the hundredth edition as an edition *de-luxe* limited to 500 copies.)

Books to which Arthur Rackham contributed Illustrations, a Frontispiece, Cover Designs or Decorations

1893

RHODES, THOMAS: *To the Other Side.*

1894

LINGWOOD, LEMMON: *The Illustrated Guide to Wells-next-the-Sea.*

BERLYN, MRS ALFRED: *Sunrise-Land: Rambles in Eastern England.* (Some of Rackham's drawings for this book were reprinted in *Pictures of East Coast Health Resorts* – undated but probably published in 1902.)

GARRETT, EDMUND: *Isis Very Much Unveiled.* (Undated but appearing from textual evidence to have been published late in 1894 or in 1895.)

IRVING, WASHINGTON: *The Sketch-Book of Geoffrey Crayon, Gent.* Holly Edition. New York and London. (This undated edition contains three illustrations by Rackham. So does the Westminster Edition, dated 1895, while the Van Tassel Edition of 1895 has four Rackham illustrations.)

1895

IRVING, WASHINGTON: *Tales of a Traveller.* New York and London.

HENLEY, W. E.: *A London Garland; selected from five centuries of English Verse.*

[SHELLEY, HENRY C.]: *The Homes and Haunts of Thomas Carlyle.*

CALVERT, WALTER: *Souvenir of Sir Henry Irving.*

1896

[FRIEDERICHS, HULDA]: *In the Evening of his Days; a Study of Mr Gladstone in Retirement.*

IRVING, WASHINGTON: *Bracebridge Hall.* New York and London.

1897

VARIOUS AUTHORS: *The 'Little Folks' Entertainment Album.*

GREG, T. T.: *Through a Glass Lightly.*

DAWE, CARLTON: *Captain Castle, a tale of the China Seas.*

1898

WEYMAN, STANLEY J.: *The Castle Inn.*

1899

NEISH, R.: *A World in a Garden.*

DEWAR, GEORGE A. B.: *Wild Life in Hampshire Highlands.* Haddon Hall Library.

HOLE, S. REYNOLDS: *Our Gardens.* Haddon Hall Library.

GRAY, SIR EDWARD: *Fly Fishing.* Haddon Hall Library.

TATE, WILLIAM J.: *East Coast Scenery.*

1900

ANONYMOUS: *Gardens Old and New.* Country Life Library.

NISBET, JAMES: *Our Forests and Woodlands.* Haddon Hall Library.

PAGET, J. OTHO: *Hunting.* Haddon Hall Library.

1901

LYTTLETON, THE HON. R. H.: *Outdoor Games; Cricket and Golf.* Haddon Hall Library.

HODDER, EDWIN: *The Life of a Century, 1800 to 1900.*

VARIOUS AUTHORS: *Queen Mab's Fairy Realm.*

GRIFFITHS, MAJOR ARTHUR: *Mysteries of Police and Crime.*

SELOUS, EDMUND: *Bird Watching.* Haddon Hall Library.

1902

BLEACKLEY, HORACE: *More Tales of the Stumps.*

SHAND, ALEXANDER INNES: *Shooting.* Haddon Hall Library.

1903

TOD, W. M.: *Farming.* Haddon Hall Library.

SPIELMANN, MRS M. H.: *Littledom Castle and other tales.*

SKETCHLEY, R. E. D.: *English Book-Illustration of To-day.*

1904

HAMER, S. H.: *The Little Folks Picture Album in Colour.*

1905

HOLME, CHARLES: *The 'Old' Water-Colour Society, 1804–1904.*

HAMILTON, MYRA: *Kingdoms Curious.*

VARIOUS AUTHORS: *The Venture; an annual, of art and literature.*

1906

HILL, MIRANDA and BROWNE, MAGGIE: *The 'Little Folks' Plays.*

VARIOUS AUTHORS: *The Children's Hour; an anthology.*

1907

TENNANT, PAMELA: *The Children and the Pictures.*

SAVORY, J. HARRY: *Auld Acquaintance; a book for friends and remembrances.*

1908

BURNS, ROBERT: *The Cotter's Saturday Night.*

VARIOUS AUTHORS: *The Odd Volume; literary and artistic.*

1909

SPIELMANN, MRS M. H.: *The Rainbow Book; tales of fun and fancy.*

1911

BALDRY, A. L.: *The Practice of Water-Colour Painting.*

1913

BEARNE, DAVID: *Boy Ballads.*
VARIOUS AUTHORS: *Faithful Friends; a collection of short stories.*
VARIOUS ARTISTS: *Pictures from Punch.* Vol. VI. (Undated but probably published in 1913.)

1914

VARIOUS AUTHORS: *King Albert's Book.*
VARIOUS AUTHORS: *Storyland, from St Nicolas.*
VARIOUS AUTHORS: *Princess Mary's Gift Book.*
HOLME, C. GEOFFREY: *Modern Book Illustrators and their work.*

1915

VARIOUS AUTHORS: *The Queen's Gift Book.*

1922

COYKENDALL, FREDERICK: *Arthur Rackham; a list of books illustrated by him.*

1923

SALAMAN, MALCOLM C.: *British Book Illustration Yesterday and To-day.*
VARIOUS AUTHORS: *The Windmill; stories, essays, poems and pictures.*

1924

VARIOUS ARTISTS: *Third Annual of Advertising Art.* New York.
BENSON, A. C. and WEAVER, SIR LAWRENCE: *The Book of the Queen's Dolls' House.*

1925

VARIOUS CONTRIBUTORS: *The Book of the Titmarsh Club.*
VARIOUS ARTISTS: *Fourth Annual of Advertising Art.* New York.

1926

FAY, ERICA: *A Road to Fairyland.*

1927

VARIOUS AUTHORS: *'Now Then!'* A volume of fact, fiction and pictures.

1928

MELVILLE, LEWIS: *Not All the Truth.*
VARIOUS AUTHORS: *A Birthday and Some Memories.* (Limited to 2,000 copies, issued to commemorate the Diamond Jubilee of the makers of 'Eno's Fruit Salts'.)
VARIOUS AUTHORS: *A New Book of Sense and Nonsense.* Edited by Ernest Rhys. Everyman's Library.

1932

VARIOUS AUTHORS: *Oxted and Limpsfield.*

1933

STARKIE, WALTER: *Raggle-Taggle.*

1934

VARIOUS AUTHORS: *The Old Water-Colour Society's Club Eleventh Annual Volume, 1933-4.* Edited by Randall Davies.
STARKIE, WALTER: *Spanish Raggle-Taggle.*

CONTRIBUTED ILLUSTRATIONS

CARROLL, WALTER: *River and Rainbow; ten miniatures for pianoforte.*

VARIOUS AUTHORS: *The Junior Book of Authors.* Edited by Stanley J. Kunitz and Howard Haycroft.

1935

THORPE, JAMES: *English Illustration: the Nineties.*

1936

STARKIE, WALTER: *Don Gypsy.*

LATIMORE, SARAH BRIGGS and HASKELL, GRACE CLARK: *Arthur Rackham: a bibliography.* Los Angeles.

1938

MACKAYE, PERCY: *The Far Familiar; fifty new poems.*

Some Periodicals containing Illustrations by Arthur Rackham or Articles by or about him

ART ET DECORATION (Paris). Jul 1912.

ARTIST AND ADVERTISER. Jan 1931.

BLACK AND WHITE. Christmas No. 1901.

BOOK MONTHLY. Christmas 1918–New Year 1919.

BOOK TRADE JOURNAL. 18 Sep, 2, 9, 16, 23 Oct, 6 13, 20, 27 Nov 1936. (The nine instalments of E. A. Osborne's 'Checklist Bibliography'.)

BOOKMAN (London). Christmas Nos. 1906, 1922, 1933; Oct 1925; Oct 1926.

BOOKMAN (New York). Feb 1908; Dec 1927.

CASSELL'S FAMILY MAGAZINE. Feb–Apr, Dec 1896; Feb, June 1897.

CASSELL'S MAGAZINE. Mar, Jul 1898; Jul, Sep, Dec 1899; Jan, Feb, Dec 1900; Feb, Aug, Sep, Oct 1901; Mar, May, Dec 1902; Feb, Mar, Dec 1903; May 1904.

CENTURY MAGAZINE. Jun 1911; Feb 1913; May, Aug, Oct 1914; Feb 1915.

CHUMS. 3 May 1893; 29 Apr 1896; 12 May, 23 Jun, 11 Aug, 6, 27 Oct, 3, 10 Nov, 15 Dec 1897; 30 Mar 1898.

CONNOISSEUR. Dec 1921.

COUNTRY. Mar, Apr 1902.

COUNTRY LIFE. 6, 13 Jan, 26 May 1900; 1 Nov 1902; 23 Jul, 27 Aug 1904; 10 Jul 1920; 13 Nov 1926.

CRAFTSMAN. Nov 1912; Dec 1914.

DAILY GRAPHIC. 27 May, 2 Jun 1890.

DAILY MIRROR. 24 Nov 1908.

DEKORATIVE KUNST (Munich). Dec 1909.

DELINEATOR (Philadelphia). Dec 1915; Jan, Dec 1916; Jul 1927.

EVERYBODY'S WEEKLY. 27 Sep 1947.

GENTLEWOMAN. 24 Mar 1900; 9 Feb 1901.

GIRL'S REALM. Nov 1908.

GOOD HOUSEKEEPING. Nov 1910; May–Nov 1925.

GRAPHIC. 16 Nov 1901; Christmas No. 1906; 23 Feb 1907.

HARMSWORTH MONTHLY PICTORIAL MAGAZINE. Jan, Feb 1899.

HORN BOOK MAGAZINE (Boston, U.S.A.). Nov–Dec 1939; May–Jun 1940.

HOUSE BEAUTIFUL (New York). Sep 1926.

ILLUSTRATED BITS. 3 Jan 1885.

ILLUSTRATED LONDON NEWS. Christmas No. 1919; 30 Sep 1933.

INTERNATIONAL STUDIO. May 1905; Feb, Jul 1923; Jan, Sep 1926.

JOURNAL (Paris). 4 Dec 1911.

LADIES' FIELD. From No. 1, 19 Mar 1898, until at least No. 353, 17 Dec 1904, various page headings designed by Rackham were used frequently.

LADIES' HOME JOURNAL (Philadelphia). Dec 1925.

LADY'S MAGAZINE. Jun, Oct, Dec 1901; Jan, Dec 1902.

LITTLE FOLKS. Feb, Mar, Apr, Jul–Dec 1896; Jan–Dec 1897; Jul–Dec 1898; Jan–Dec 1899; Jan–Dec 1900; Jan–Dec 1901; Jan–Dec 1902; Jan–Dec 1903; Jul–Dec 1904; Jan–Dec 1905; Jan 1906; Oct 1907.

LONDON BOOKMAN. Oct 1925; Oct 1926.

LONDON MAGAZINE. Dec 1903; Jan, Feb, Mar, Apr, May, Jul, Oct 1904; Apr, June 1905.

MAGAZINE OF ART. Jun 1903.

MORNING POST. 1 Feb 1910.

NAVY AND ARMY ILLUSTRATED. 24 Dec 1897 to 8 Oct 1898. (A headpiece, repeated fortnightly.)

PALL MALL BUDGET. 15, 22 Jan, 5, 12, 26 Feb, 5, 12, 19, 26 Mar, 2, 16 Apr, 9, 16 Jul, 6, 27 Aug, 3, 10, 24 Sep, 1, 8 Oct, 17, 31 Dec 1891; 7, 14, 21, 28 Jan, 4, 11, 18, 25 Feb, 3, 10, 17, 31 Mar, 14, 21, 28 Apr, 5, 12, 26 May, 2, 23, 30 Jun, 7, 14, 21 Jul, 15, 22, 29 Sep, 13, 27 Oct, 10, 17 Nov, 1, 15, 22, 29 Dec 1892.

PALL MALL MAGAZINE. Dec 1905; Jan, Feb 1906.

PEARSON'S MAGAZINE. Aug 1902.

PUNCH. Almanacks for 1905, 1906, 1907, 1913. 30 Aug, 6, 27 Sep, 11, 25 Oct, 15, 29 Nov 1905; 3 Jan, 14 Feb 1906; 3 Jan 1934.

QUIVER. Feb 1897; Mar 1898.

ST NICHOLAS MAGAZINE. Dec 1912; Jan, Apr, Jun, Jul, Aug, Sep, Oct, Dec 1913; Feb, Mar, May, Jun, Jul, Aug, Oct, Nov, Dec 1914.

SCRAPS. 4 Oct, 15 Nov 1884; 3 Jan 1885.

SCRIBNER'S MAGAZINE (New York). Oct 1904; Feb 1906; Aug 1907.

SPHERE. 27 Nov 1909, 6 Jan 1934.

STUDIO. 15 Sep 1904; 15 Apr, Special Spring No. 1905; Vol LXVI 1916; Mar 1923.

SURREY TIMES. 1 Mar 1892.

TIME (New York). 8 Nov 1926.

TRAVELLER. 27 Apr, 8 Jun 1901.

WESTMINSTER BUDGET. 2 Feb 1893 and frequently until Dec 1896.

WIDE WORLD MAGAZINE. Jul 1901.

WOMAN'S HOME COMPANION. Dec 1931.

WOMAN'S JOURNAL. Dec 1929.

Some Ephemera
with designs by Arthur Rackham

ADVERTISEMENTS.

Coloured drawings for Colgate's Cashmere Bouquet Soap, used in *Ladies' Home Journal*, *Pictorial Review*, *Vogue*, *Asia* and *Good Housekeeping* in 1923–5 and incorporated into window-display stands.

Black-and-white drawing for Eno's Fruit Salts, used in *Punch*, 11th July 1928.

Coloured drawing for Cadbury's Chocolates, used on chocolate-box lids, 1933.

BOOKPLATES.

Arthur Rackham. (For his own set of the books he illustrated.)

Barbara Mary Rackham. (For his daughter.)

G. L. Lazarus. (Commissioned by a collector.)

Robert Partridge. (Commissioned by a collector.)

CATALOGUES.

The Illustrations of Arthur Rackham. Heinemann (*c.* 1910). (A folded leaflet advertising six books.)

The North Wall. Argus Book Shop, Chicago. Fall, 1933.

The Best Books of the Season 1933–4. Simpkin Marshall, Ltd (1933).

The Best Books of the Season 1935–6. Simpkin Marshall, Ltd (1935).

Costume Through the Ages; a series of six water-colour drawings. Maggs Bros., Ltd (1938).

Catalogue of the Arthur Rackham Memorial Exhibition. Leicester Galleries. December 1939.

(There have been numerous exhibitions of Rackham's drawings, for most of which unillustrated catalogues were issued. Notable exhibitions were held at the Leicester Galleries, London, in 1905, 1906, 1908, 1935 and 1939; at Scott and Fowles', New York, in 1919, 1920, 1922 and 1927; and at Columbia University, New York, in 1956–7.)

CHRISTMAS CARDS.

Arthur Rackham frequently used personal greetings cards either specially designed by him or incorporating a design made for one of his books. Greetings cards for the following years are known:

1900, 1906, 1908, 1909, 1910, 1911, 1912, 1919, 1926, 1930, 1931, 1932, 1934.

Private greetings cards with designs by Arthur Rackham were produced for Sir George Savage and his family at Christmas 1910, 1911, 1912 and three unspecified years.

A Christmas brochure produced in U.S.A. for Mr and Mrs John Barry Ryan, in 1932, has a coloured illustration by Rackham mounted on the front wrapper.

A drawing of an old bookshop, originally printed in the *Pall Mall Budget* for 28th January 1892, was reproduced as a private greetings card in 1958 for Mr and Mrs R. A. Brimmell.

DUST-WRAPPERS.

Several books illustrated by Arthur Rackham were issued in coloured dust-wrappers specially designed or incorporating extra decoration not used in the book. The following are known examples:
A Christmas Carol. 1915
Comus. 1921
A Dish of Apples. 1921
Poor Cecco. 1925
The Legend of Sleepy Hollow. 1928
The Compleat Angler. 1931
Fairy Tales by Hans Andersen. 1932
The Arthur Rackham Fairy Book. 1933
Poe's Tales of Mystery and Imagination. 1935
Peer Gynt. 1936

INVITATION CARDS.

For the Private View of an Exhibition of Water Colour Drawings illustrating *Rip Van Winkle*, and other Fantasies, on 11th March 1905, at the Leicester Galleries, Leicester Square.

For a Conversazione of the Artists' Society and the Langham Sketching Club. 23rd February 1906.

MENU.

For the Seventh Dinner of the Titmarsh Club. 14th November 1909.

NEWSPAPER SUPPLEMENT.

Liverpool Shipping Telegraph and Daily Commercial Advertiser. Supplement. 25th May 1895.
(A single sheet, 22 by 17 inches, with 14 illustrations for an article on the new Baltic and North Sea Canal.)

PROGRAMME.

For a concert at the St John's Wood Art Club. 5th April 1909.

SELF-PORTRAIT.

A pen-and-ink sketch of the artist at work, drawn for E. A. Osborne. 1938. (Never published. A block was made and two proofs were pulled in 1938. One is in the possession of Mr Osborne and the other in the G. L. Lazarus collection.)

WEDDING ANNOUNCEMENTS.

A folio sheet reproduced in facsimile, being an illustrated jocular testimonial accompanying a wedding gift (to Maggie Browne). 1896.

A card announcing the marriage and new address of Philip Soper and Barbara Rackham. 1935.